A Look at Psychology

WHY WE DO WHAT WE DO

By Elizabeth Hall

HOUGHTON MIFFLIN COMPANY BOSTON 1973

Also by
ELIZABETH HALL

Phoebe Snow
Stand Up, Lucy

9911

Library of Congress Cataloging in Publication Data

Hall, Elizabeth, 1929-
   Why we do what we do.

   1. Psychology--Juvenile literature.
I. Title.
BF149.5.H3   150   73-8844
ISBN 0-395-17516-X

FIRST PRINTING   V

CONTENTS

For Susan and David

Preface

NOT MANY YEARS AGO, schools refused to teach the elements of psychology to young people. Most college freshmen were considered too "immature" to enroll in the introductory psychology class.

In the past twenty-five years, psychology has moved from the colleges and universities to the elementary schools. Today fourth graders learn the elements of operant conditioning. We have discovered that the principles that underlie much of psychology are simple and understandable, not complex and mysterious.

The field of psychology is vast, and attempts to compress it into a single small book make many omissions necessary. One thing I have tried to stress is the lack of final knowledge in most areas, from memory and language to attitude change and aggression. Disagreements run deep, and cherished theories may disappear as further research produces more accurate knowledge. Psychologist D. O. Hebb once said of his own cell-assembly system, "It is not true. A good theory is one that holds together long enough to get you to a better theory."

This book would have been impossible without the assistance of three psychologists who read every word of the first draft and made valuable suggestions: Paul Chance, Joyce Dudney Fleming, and Carol Tavris. Nor could I have finished it without Scott O'Dell, who patiently read and warned me whenever I lapsed into jargon. I would also like to thank Jerome S. Bruner, who read the chapters on common sense and on culture; James V. McConnell, who read the chapter on memory; and D. O. Hebb, who read the chapters on memory and on language. Their words of encouragement were important.

Why We Do What We Do

Psychology and Common Sense

1

PSYCHOLOGY TOUCHES every part of your life. Your choice of toothpaste, the way you remember a telephone number, your ability to ride a bicycle, the kind of people you like, how you express your anger, the occupation you choose, the girl or boy you find attractive, and even why you get out of bed in the morning have all been studied by psychologists. Psychology asks why man behaves the way he does — and then tries to find out.

The simplest definition of psychology is "the science of behavior." Psychologists believe that there are laws of human behavior that can be discovered and then used to predict other human behavior.

Most behavior is obvious: a person sleeps, walks, eats, works, goes to school, watches television, dances, swims, makes love, talks, paints a picture, fights, plays a guitar. But some behavior can be detected only with instruments: brain waves, heart and breathing changes, eye movements, electric charges on the skin. And still other behavior cannot be measured directly: feelings, perceptions, thoughts, memories, and motives. Psychologists have to make guesses about this inner behavior, guesses that are based upon behavior they can observe or measure and upon what they know about the behavior that goes on inside their own bodies. This educated guessing is called *inference*.

All of us use inference every day. Suppose you and your friend both look at a stoplight. You say that the light is red and your friend agrees. How do you know that you are seeing the same color? When your friend says that the light is red, you infer that he is seeing the same color you see. Most of the time your inference will be right. But not always. If your friend is male, there is roughly one chance in ten that he has some form of colorblindness, and red-green colorblindness is the common form.

If your friend happened to be a colorblind male, and you took him into a laboratory to match colors, you would soon find that red and green look the same to him. He may not know that he is colorblind; until about three hundred years ago no one knew that colorblindness existed. But he knows that a stoplight is red because all his life people have told him so. He interprets the color he sees when he looks at a stoplight as red.

Although psychology is a new field of study, man has always tried to explain human behavior. For centuries, astrologers explained a person's character by the position of the stars in the heavens at the moment of his birth. They predicted his behavior by the changing relation of the stars and the planets. Others believed that a person's physical appearance determined his behavior. If a man looked like a fox, he would be sly and crafty.

A hundred years ago, many people believed that the shapes and sizes of bumps on a person's skull revealed his character. A large bump over the left temple, for example, meant that a person had a keen sense of humor; above the left ear, it might indicate thrift.

Not all the ways man has explained human behavior are so strange. He has watched people, applied his common sense to their actions, and developed a series of guides to behavior that we call *proverbs*. These sayings, handed down from generation to generation, sound plausible. An entire book of the Bible is filled with them. You have probably used many of them yourself.

When we try to use proverbs as a guide to character or to predict conduct, we find that we are in trouble. They contradict each other. "You can't teach an old dog new tricks," we say. But we also say, "You're never too old to learn." "Look before you leap," warns a friend, when you plan to run for class president against the most popular boy in school. Another friend has a different idea: "He who hesitates is lost." You can't follow both proverbs at once. Common sense is not always wrong, but its wisdom often contradicts itself. Psychology tries to develop principles of human behavior that do not conflict, principles that are *consistent*.

Common sense often advises us to do different things because it is so vague. The terms are so general that they apply to opposite situations and predict opposite results. Suppose your closest friend of the opposite sex is moving to another town. You have been inseparable for a year and have planned to go to the same small college together. Will you remain close and carry out your plans? "Certainly," you say; "Absence makes the heart grow fonder."

Afterward, when your friend has forgotten you, you will say wisely, "I should have known; Out of sight, out of mind." But now you are using hindsight, choosing the proverb that fits a known outcome. Common sense does not take conditions into account. It does not specify what will happen if your friend meets an attractive new person, or if you exchange few letters or phone calls, or if your friend develops interests that are totally different from the ones you shared.

Psychologists try to define their terms carefully and spell out the conditions under which their theories will work. They want to predict behavior, not just explain it.

Psychologists constantly ask *why*. Common sense pays as little attention to explaining human behavior as cave men paid to explaining fire. The cave man knew that fire burned; it gave off warmth; it cooked food; and it was dangerous. But he did not try to find out that fire resulted when oxygen combined rapidly with combustible materials. Nor could he tell you just how this process rearranged atoms into new substances.

In the same way, common sense tells us that if we want to memorize a list of French words, we must study them. Everybody knows that. The psychologist goes further. He studies memory in the hope of discovering what chemical changes in the brain and nervous system must take place before you can remember that *pas ce soir* means "not tonight."

When your father says, "All work and no play makes Jack a dull boy," or, "A fool and his money are soon parted," he is stating a common-sense principle of human behavior. Most parents and teachers believe in these principles and pass them on as good advice. Because they make sense, we nod our heads and tell them to others. Some proverbs are true in most cases; some are probably true in some cases; and some — like "Spare the rod and spoil the child" — may never be true.

The only way to find out if they are right is to test them in a systematic manner. Proverbs never get this kind of test, and so we go on believing them. Perhaps we see one example that upholds a proverb and so we continue to trust it. But we have no reports on large numbers of cases to tell us that 85 out of

100 fools soon lose their money — nor do we even have a strict definition of a fool.

When psychologists put forth a principle of human behavior, they try to word it so that it can be tested under strict conditions. The results of this testing are *data*. Sometimes the data produced by critical, systematic testing disprove a principle that looks right to common sense, and sometimes the testing confirms common sense.

All the differences between psychology and common sense are also the differences between common sense and science. Psychologists apply the methods of science to the behavior of animals and people. This means that psychologists must design experiments that can test their theories. Suppose, for example, that you wanted to find out if some animals can recognize their own images in mirrors. We know that some fish and birds and dogs react to their reflections as if they believed that the creatures in the mirrors were other fish and birds and dogs. Often a dog will growl and bark at its image in a mirror, and at least one kind of bird will attack its reflection in the shiny hubcap of a parked car. If you could find an animal that learned to recognize itself in a mirror, you would likely have an animal with a high intelligence — an intelligence different from most animals' and more like man's.

A psychologist named Gordon Gallup put chimpanzees in cages by themselves, where they could not see other chimps. Every day he put a full-length mirror outside each cage and left it there for eight hours. At first the chimps acted as if they were looking at other chimpanzees, but after a few days they began to act just as human beings do when they look into a mirror. They picked their teeth or their noses and inspected parts of their bodies.

Gallup was sure that the chimpanzees recognized themselves, but he had to devise a way to test his belief. He anesthetized the chimps and, while they were unconscious, daubed a harmless red dye on the upper edge of one eyebrow and the ear on the opposite side of their heads. The dye had no odor, so the chimps could not detect it by smell. And Gallup had painted the dye on himself to make sure that it could not be felt after it dried.

When the chimps were awake and back in their cages, Gallup watched them carefully. They seemed unaware of the red dye on their ears and eyebrows. Then the full-length mirrors were set up in front of the cages. The chimps became excited, peered at their reflections, and touched the red patches on their heads. One chimp even smelled its fingers after touching its ear.

To be sure that the chimps recognized themselves in the mirrors, Gallup repeated his experiment with two chimpanzees that had never seen a mirror before. Daubed with dye and placed before mirrors, they acted as if they were looking at other chimpanzees. Not once did they touch their red patches.

Just watching those first chimpanzees in front of mirrors had convinced Gallup that they recognized themselves in the reflections. But there was always a chance that their responses to the images were accidents. He had to devise a way to test his theory, and it had to be a test that other psychologists could repeat. Then, to make sure that the chimps touched the red marks because they recognized themselves in the mirrors, and not because the dye tickled or itched or felt stiff, he tested the two chimpanzees that had not learned about mirrors.

Gallup later tested several kinds of monkeys in the same way, but not one of them learned to recognize its own reflection. This simple experiment indicates that the intelligence of apes — in this case, chimpanzees — is different in some way from the intelligence of monkeys, and that apes perhaps share with man the concept of *self*.

You may wonder why psychologists bother to study the behavior of animals. Many psychologists never work with human beings, but spend their time studying rats, pigeons, monkeys, dogs, bats, flies, fish, or worms. Learning to understand animal behavior is a good reason for studying any animal. But there are even better reasons.

It is much easier to control the conditions surrounding animals than to control a human being's surroundings. A person leaves the laboratory and returns to other surroundings, or an *environment*, very different from the controlled situation in the laboratory. An animal may spend its entire life without ever leaving the laboratory.

Many experiments cannot be carried out with human subjects. For example, suppose you wanted to know what would happen if a person never saw other human beings from the time he was born. You could not take babies from their mothers and keep them away from all other people. But you could raise rats or chimpanzees or dogs that never had contact with other rats or chimpanzees or dogs, and in this way you might discover what kinds of behavior a particular animal must learn by watching others of its kind.

Some animals have a very short life span, and within a few years psychologists can follow behavior in a group over several generations. This helps them learn how a culture changes over the years. They can also breed animals that have traits they want to study. This is a good way to find out what characteristics are inherited.

Since animals are not as complex as human beings, their behavior is simpler than that of people and easier to study. Psychologists can try to separate a single aspect of behavior and study it, by controlling other influences.

Sometimes the study of animals tells us much about man, but psychologists are careful about applying the results of animal experiments directly to human behavior. Sometimes animals and people react in different ways. The theories that come out of animal research give other psychologists ideas and theories that can lead to human experiments and new knowledge about human behavior.

Psychologists can test few theories with just one experiment. It took several tries, each changing the situation in some way, before Gallup was satisfied that chimpanzees can learn to recognize themselves in mirrors. The two chimps that had never before seen mirrors were an important part of the experiment. They formed what psychologists call a *control group.* A control group is made up of subjects — animals or persons — that undergo the same testing but do not have the original experience the psychologist hopes to test.

All scientists use control groups. For example, if a drug researcher wanted to test a new cold remedy, he would give the medicine to a group of people suffering from colds. At the same time, he would give plain sugar pills to a control group of people with colds. If the people in the control group got well as fast as those who had taken the new medicine, the researcher would assume that his remedy had little or no effect on colds.

Sometimes even carefully planned experiments are difficult to interpret. Most of us obey the orders of our bosses or teachers or police officers or other officials. During World War II, millions of innocent persons died in European death camps, and thousands of honest German citizens helped kill them because the German government commanded them to do so. The German who worked in a death camp believed that he was moral and law-abiding; he followed the orders of his government. In the same way, soldiers who shoot civilians in time of war are following the orders of their officers.

Obedience can lead man into terrible crimes, but without obedience there could be no society of any kind. If no one obeyed the laws, none of us would have food or shelter or clothing, and we would live in a constant state of fear. Because obedience leads to both good and wicked acts, psychologist Stanley Milgram decided to study it. He wondered how many persons would obey orders even when they were told to commit acts that clearly were wrong.

He asked a group of men to take part in a learning experiment. The men believed that Milgram wanted to study the effect of punishment on memory. They thought the experiment was designed to find out if pain helps people learn and just how much pain makes people learn best.

In the study, two men came into the laboratory at a time. The experimenter asked them to draw lots to decide who would be the "teacher" and who would be the "learner." The learner was taken to another room and strapped into an electric chair. The teacher sat before a generator and — on orders of the experimenter — threw switches that delivered electric shocks to the learner when he made a mistake in memorizing pairs of words.

The experimenter told the men that the shocks would be painful but not dangerous. However, the instrument panel was clearly marked with information that contradicted the experimenter. A label above each of the thirty switches gave the voltage that the switch delivered, and each group of four switches carried a description such as *Slight Shock* or *Moder-*

ate Shock. Toward the end of the row, four switches were labeled *Danger: Severe Shock*, and the last two switches were marked *XXX*.

When the teacher threw a switch, a small red light went on, the generator buzzed, a blue light flashed, the dial on the voltage meter swung to the right, and the machine produced a series of clicks. Each time the learner gave a wrong answer, the experimenter ordered the teacher to increase the voltage so that the shock was stronger and more painful. Milgram wanted to find out at what point the teacher would disobey and refuse to give further painful or dangerous shocks to a fellow human being.

The teacher did not know that the drawing was rigged — both slips of paper said "teacher" — and that the "learner" was a stooge of the experimenter. There was no electric current and the learner got no shocks at all. The answers and actions of the learner were the same in each experiment, because the learner was following the experimenter's script. As the teacher increased the shock past 300 volts, the learner pounded on the wall of his room, and the teacher could hear the pounding.

At 315 volts the learner refused to answer, and the teacher usually asked the experimenter for instructions. The experimenter always told the teacher to treat silence as a wrong answer and to increase the shocks. Again the learner pounded on the wall, and again the teacher increased the voltage. For the rest of the experiment, the learner remained ominously silent. He neither answered nor pounded.

In one series of these experiments, 65 percent of the teachers kept increasing the shock to the highest possible voltage — 450 volts, a level clearly marked *XXX* and six stages past the level marked *Danger: Severe Shock*. Only about 13 percent of the teachers refused to go on with the experiment after the first protest from the learner. Another 22 percent stopped before they reached the most dangerous levels.

The teachers in the experiments showed that they believed the excessive shocks were wrong. They trembled, sweated, stuttered, bit their lips, groaned, and dug their fingernails into their flesh. But they continued to administer what they thought were painful and perhaps lethal shocks to the learner.

Milgram repeated these experiments many times, changing the script so that the learner screamed and begged for help, moving the location away from the university setting, paying or not paying the teacher, placing the teacher where he could see the learner writhing in pain. But no matter how he changed the situation, a surprisingly large number of people went on to the end, throwing the switches for the 450-volt shock.

Our first look at these results plunges us into despair. They seem to say that 65 percent of the people would — if ordered — kill their fellow men. But the situation is not that simple. When we look at the experiment carefully, we find circumstances that would not apply in most real-life situations.

The laboratory was located at a famous university, and the teachers may have believed that any study sponsored by the university was safe, no matter how dangerous it appeared. When Milgram repeated his study away from the campus, another 17 percent refused to pull the switches. As soon as the experiment lost the protection of the university, the number of people willing to obey to the end dropped to 48 percent.

The teachers knew that, because they had volunteered for the experiment, the learners also had volunteered. They believed it was only chance that put them before the generator instead of in the electric chair.

Most important, the teachers believed that the experiment

was important, one that would advance scientific knowledge and help mankind. They trusted the experimenter to design a safe experiment, and they had been told that the shocks would be painful but not dangerous.

Perhaps this experiment teaches us that most persons trust scientists and will do whatever scientists ask them to do. The past century has been one of humane scientific achievement, and most persons believe that the psychologist cares for his fellow man. (And they were right in this case. There *was* no danger to the learner.)

All these factors probably added to the number of persons who threw switches to the bitter end. It was impossible to design the experiment so no outside factors influenced it. But even an imperfect experiment can tell us a lot. After we allow for all these excuses, we are left with the uneasy knowledge that too many people will obey even when obedience conflicts with their moral code. In the most extreme of the experiments, when the teacher (who was insulated from the current) had to force the screaming learner's hand onto the voltage plate, 30 percent threw the switch to deliver the final, fatal shock. Like good Germans or good soldiers, these people put the responsibility on the authorities and thought of themselves — not as murderers — but as good citizens carrying out orders.

Not all psychologists conduct their research in laboratories. Some researchers go out among people and ask them questions about behavior and attitudes. They take the results back to their offices and use computers to analyze the answers. They may compare the answers they get with the different characteristics of the people who answered. Age, sex, education, income, and religion are among the first ways they divide the answers.

Sometimes the amount of education a person has affects his

attitudes and beliefs. For example, when the National Commission on the Causes and Prevention of Violence surveyed the American people, it found that nearly two-thirds of those who never graduated from high school believed that justice worked better in the vigilante days of the Old West than it does now. Only one-third of those with college educations agreed with them.

Psychologists cannot ask each person in the country how he feels about violence or whom he will support for president or whether he believes in capital punishment. Some people must represent all the people in such a survey. The people who answer the questions are called the *sample,* and, in order to get reliable answers, researchers must make sure that the sample represents the whole country.

If psychologists interview only men or only college students or only people from New York City, their data will tell them what men feel about violence, but not what women feel; whom college students support for president, but not whom the voters are likely to elect; whether New Yorkers believe capital punishment should be abolished, but not what the rest of the country believes.

Once his research is complete and his data give him the same strong answer each time he repeats his experiments, the psychologist feels ready to explain some small aspect of human or animal behavior. He may go even further and predict what other persons or other animals are likely to do if they find themselves in situations similar to the ones he studied.

You may feel that no one will ever be able to predict what you will do tomorrow or next week, or how you feel about persons with different skins or different religions. No one, of course, can look at you and predict your actions or attitudes accurately. But the more a psychologist knows about your background, the more likely he is to be right in his predictions.

Much human behavior is already predictable. We all predict behavior every day; we gamble our lives on it. When the surgeon begins to take out your appendix, you predict that the scalpel will not slip. When the light turns red, you predict that the cars will stop so that you can cross the street with safety. When you play with your fierce-looking German shepherd, you predict that he will not bite you. When you buy mushrooms at the grocery store, you predict that the grower knows the difference between mushrooms and toadstools. When you get on an airplane, you predict that the pilot will not crash when he tries to land.

Data from experiments and from surveys among the people confirm theories that predict how most of us will behave. Not every subject will respond the same way in each experiment. The psychologist works with probabilities, not with certainties, and his predictions are generally accurate when he applies them to a large group. In the same way, the physicist's predictions about the action of atomic particles are true for the millions of particles in a chamber, but he cannot point to a single neutron and tell you how it will move.

Through their studies, psychologists hope to help solve personal and social problems. With a more accurate knowledge of human behavior, you would be able to study better, to choose a career or a marriage partner more wisely, to live a happier life. And if we all knew more about human behavior, we might come closer to solving the problems of crime, poverty, prejudice, and war.

Cultural Backgrounds

2

N OT TOO MANY years ago, when they heard the word *culture*, most people thought of music, painting, sculpture, poetry, theater, philosophy, religion, and perhaps the sciences. Social scientists use the word in a different way, and their definition has begun to replace the traditional meaning we gave to culture. Psychologists and other social scientists consider that culture includes all the ways people in a particular society behave and think. This way of looking at culture includes all the old meanings of the word and adds to it everything from the food the people eat — and the way they eat it — to the way they light fires, elect mayors, and make naughty children mind.

From the moment a baby is born, his culture begins to influence him and helps to determine the way he will behave as an adult. If you had been born in Moscow or in Calcutta or in Cairo, you would be a very different person from the one who is reading this book.

Anthropology is the science devoted to the study of cultures. There are some areas where psychologists and anthropologists work together to understand how a society shapes the attitudes and behavior of its members. In order to understand a single member of a society, psychologists must understand what the society expects of him and whether he lives up to those expectations.

Culture shapes behavior that most of us consider natural. In the United States, for example, we think that men are naturally aggressive, independent, and reasonable. We think that women are gentle, cooperative, loving, and emotional. But anthropologists have found societies in which both men and women are like U.S. men, societies in which both men and women behave like U.S. women, and societies in which men act like American women and women act like American men.

In this country, boy babies and girl babies are treated differently. Clothes for the tiniest babies are generally different for boys and for girls. Manufacturers put lace and ruffles on clothes meant for baby girls and tailor clothes for baby boys in a masculine fashion. This kind of clothing signals the sex of a baby to even a casual visitor. And we respond to those signals.

The next time you see someone playing with a baby, watch closely. Many persons encourage a boy baby to be tough and aggressive before he can sit up. They double up his tiny fists and pretend to box with him. They bring him rattles shaped like boxing gloves or baseball bats. As soon as he can walk, they take away his stuffed toys and give him trucks and cars, toy soldiers, guns, and sports equipment. His sister gets to keep her stuffed animals, is given dolls, tea sets, and miniature irons, stoves, and washing machines.

When psychologists visited mothers and babies in their homes, they found that the mothers treated their twelve-week-old girl and boy babies differently. The mothers looked at their baby girls more and talked to them more than they talked to their baby boys. But until they were six months old, boys were touched and held more than girls.

The same psychologists who visited the babies when they

were three months old and again when they were six months old set up an observation room in their laboratory. They asked the mothers to bring their babies into the lab after the babies had reached their first birthdays. Each mother took her baby into the observation room and sat in a chair while her baby played with toys that lay scattered about the room. After fifteen minutes, Michael Lewis and his colleagues placed a fence across the middle of the room to separate the mother and her baby.

Boys played more roughly with their toys than girls did, banging the toys together. Boys also played with light switches or doorknobs instead of spending all their time with the toys. When the fence separated the babies from their mothers, girls stood in the middle of the room and cried, while boys tried to get around the fence.

It would be easy to assume that the children played differently because boys are naturally different from girls. But Lewis watched the way the mothers behaved with their children. Usually the mother discouraged her boy from touching her or playing next to her. She would point out something in the room to catch the boy's attention or suggest that he play with a toy that lay some distance from her chair. Most girl babies were allowed to spend the fifteen minutes playing near their mothers or touching them.

Babies *respond* to adults by imitating the behavior they see. In other words, what the parent does to the baby, the baby is likely to do back. It seems that mothers teach their boys to be more independent and more aggressive than girls simply by moving them away whenever they get too close.

Lewis suggests that mothers believe boys should be more independent than girls and should be encouraged to explore and master their world. That is the standard our culture holds up for men, and mothers encourage their baby boys to follow it. This experiment does not prove that there are no basic differences between girls and boys, but it shows how a culture develops differences.

When these babies grow up and have children of their own, they will — in the same way — pass along the same cultural standards. Parents are not the only teachers of growing children, though. Baby sitters, relatives, books, television, movies, church, school, and other children all teach the child his proper role as prescribed by his culture. He learns the role so gradually and with so little effort that he tends to forget just how much of his behavior is learned — and how much of it would be different if he lived in another society.

Our culture determines even what we see. One psychologist, J. W. Bagby, asked a group of Mexican and American school teachers to look into a device and tell him what they saw. The device presented a different picture to each eye. One eye saw a baseball player and the other eye saw a bullfighter. When Bagby asked the teachers what they saw, most of the Americans said they saw a baseball player and most of the Mexicans said they saw a bullfighter.

A group of anthropologists showed a famous illusion to the Todas of India:

To most people, one of these lines appears to be longer than the other. Actually, both lines are the same length, and that is just how they looked to the Todas. The illusion was no illusion in their eyes. When the anthropologists made wooden models of the illusion, however, the people of this Indian society were fooled by the three-dimensional models. One rod looked longer than the other, just as it did to the anthropologists. In the Todas' culture, there are no photographs, no paintings, no drawings. The eyes of the Todas are just like ours, but their society has not trained them to look at a picture and connect it with a solid, three-dimensional object.

If we want to be correct, we should say that people in different cultures notice different things, not that they see different things. Language often reveals what a culture believes is important and what its members learn to notice. An Arab has 6000 words that refer to a camel. That may seem odd, but try putting down all the words you know that refer to a car. The list would fill pages. The camel is important in the Arab's life, and he sees differences among camels that our eyes do not notice. To the Arab, most cars look alike. But cars are important in our society, and our eyes are trained to notice small differences.

Members of the same culture share many beliefs. They express these beliefs about the world in their religion, in such ceremonies as baptisms, marriages and funerals, and in literature and painting. Young members of the culture learn these beliefs from hearing the culture's myths, from watching the ceremonies, and from looking at the paintings.

Beliefs affect behavior in many ways. People in some cultures believe that the gods have forbidden them to do certain things. They believe that if they break the laws of the gods, they will die. In our own culture, people of many religions believe that if they break the laws of God, they will be punished after they die.

Different cultures have different values. They believe their members should aim at different goals, with the result that what is valued highly in one society may be of little importance in another. The Navajos, in the southwestern United States, value beauty. Through their language, their customs, and their religion, Navajos learn to seek and enjoy beauty in many forms: in song and dance, in sand painting, in weaving, in decorative pottery, and in intricate silver work.

Navajos do not value material success. They think it is wrong to devote one's life to getting rich. A Navajo stops accumulating possessions as soon as he has enough for comfort. The Navajo idea of reasonable wealth is good clothes and a fine horse, but owning clothes and horses gives credit to the Navajo's family and not to the Navajo himself.

A Navajo does not want to be a leader, because no Navajo will make decisions for a group. Navajo decisions are not made until everyone in the group agrees. Such a set of values conflicts with those of the larger American culture that urges every boy to strive to be President of the United States — or at least to get rich.

Economic and technical progress are difficult if the practices of a culture stand in the way. In Greece, the family is extremely important, and children learn to love all their relatives and be loyal to them. But they also learn to dislike and suspect persons who are not related to them. Greek children mind their parents and accept their orders without question. But they do not learn to accept orders from outsiders. His parents tell the Greek child that he is the smartest, bravest, handsomest person ever born.

After studying Greek culture, psychologists Harry and Pola Triandis pointed out that the way children are brought up in Greece helps to explain why Greece has had trouble developing technology. Because he is suspicious of outsiders, a Greek finds it difficult to cooperate in large groups. Because he doesn't really believe his parents' assurances that he is the most wonderful person on earth, a Greek doubts his own worth. Even so, he behaves for the world as if his parents' praises were true. As a result, he can't take criticism. Because he accepts his parents' words as law, a Greek finds it hard to adopt new ways of doing things. Because he can accept only the authority of his parents, a Greek finds it difficult to work for an employer.

The Triandises say that Greece cannot accept Western business practices until Greeks change the ways they treat their children. These psychologists do not say that Greek child-rearing practices are wrong and that American practices are right. They say only that Greek practices stand in the way of what Greece says it wants to do.

Not everyone in a society follows all the customs of that society all the time. Occasionally you will see a right-handed American eat as Europeans do, holding his fork in his left hand. And most Americans who visit Chinese restaurants are willing to try eating with chopsticks. A society pays little attention to such violations of customs — although the diners in a Western-style restaurant would whisper or stare at someone who used chopsticks to eat his steak and baked potato.

There are certain kinds of customs, however, that a society does not permit its members to break. These customs are called *norms*, and breaking them threatens the structure of the society. When a person violates a norm, the rest of the society punishes him. Many norms are backed up by laws. In our society, it would violate both a norm and the law if a brother married his sister or a father married his daughter.

Not all members of a society adopt the values of their society. There are some Greeks who welcome new ways of doing things and some Navajos who want to be rich, just as there are some Americans who don't care about material success and some who spend their lives seeking beauty. But most persons conform to most of society's customs and values most of the time.

No society can make all its members behave exactly alike. Each person is different at birth. A baby begins life as a single, tiny cell that weighs only one twenty-millionth of an ounce. Inside that first cell is a chemical blueprint for life: the *genes* and *chromosomes* that will shape the development of a human being.

Chromosomes are threadlike bodies made up of proteins, DNA (deoxyribonucleic acid), and RNA (ribonucleic acid). That first cell, like every cell in the body of the developed human being, has forty-six chromosomes. Chromosomes always go in pairs, and one member of each pair comes from the father, while the other comes from the mother. Genes, which are located along the strands of the chromosomes, carry the specific traits — such as red hair or blue eyes — that will make up the new human being.

Your neighbor may say, "Jimmy got his quick temper from his father," but it is unlikely that the temper came along in the genes Jimmy got from his father. It would be nearer the truth to say that Jimmy picked up his quick temper from living with his father and watching his father lose his temper again and again.

For many years people have argued over whether certain personality traits are learned or inherited. This battle is called the *nature-nurture controversy*. Those who believe that your personality — which includes your intelligence and your ways of behaving — is inherited are on the side of nature. Those who believe that your personality is the result of your experience in life are on the nurture side.

Psychologists who work with inherited traits are called behavior geneticists. The fact that they study behavior shows they believe that the genes we inherit affect the ways we behave. But it is impossible to take human beings away from their daily life, or to decide which men to breed with which women in order to study the effects of selected breeding on people.

It is much easier for behavior geneticists to study animals with short life spans. They can control the mating of these animals and try to find out if genes do indeed affect behavior. One psychologist studied a group of rats that were learning to run through mazes to reach food. A maze is a long, narrow box that gives a rat a choice of pathways. If it makes the wrong turn, the rat will not be able to reach the food that the psychologist has placed at the end of the maze.

R. C. Tryon mated with each other rats that learned to find food quickly, and he mated with each other rats that had trouble finding food. Then he mated the children of bright rats with other children of bright rats, and the children of dull rats with other children of dull rats. He did this for eight generations of rats, so that the last rats he tested were the great-great-great-great-great grandchildren of the first rats.

Each generation of bright rats did better than their parents, and each generation of dull rats did worse. At last, the bright rats usually made about 25 false tries in 19 trips through the lengthy maze, while the dull rats usually made about 125 wrong turns in 19 trips. We can say that the ability that helps a rat learn to figure out a maze is largely inherited.

But even inherited traits combine with life conditions, or the *environment*, to produce the adult rat or the adult human being. One psychologist has said that asking whether an ability like intelligence is inherited is like asking which determines the area of a field — the length or the width. One is just as important as the other.

Another psychologist studied hoarding in mice that had been bred for twenty generations to develop this trait. Marvin Manosevitz developed mice that were misers, and he also found out that the kind of environment the mice lived in affected the amount of grain they hoarded. After studying the mice carefully, he estimated that about one third to one half of the hoarding in his mice was due to genetic influence. And he had developed these mice by breeding mouse misers to each other for twenty generations.

We can say that each person begins life with his own set of inherited characteristics that will affect the way he behaves. We can also say that our environment is at least as important as our genetic inheritance.

A person's physical appearance affects his behavior. If he is taller, stronger, or handsomer than most persons around him, he will behave differently from those who resemble persons around them. And his behavior will be markedly different from those who are shorter, weaker, or less attractive than the people they associate with.

One family may teach customs and values differently from another. Or a family may be broken by divorce or death, so that a child suddenly finds himself in a new situation that makes him behave differently. Because of their different backgrounds, two persons may interpret a cultural norm differently. While their behavior will not be similar, each will stay within the norm.

Unless a society is shut off from the rest of the world, the arrival of immigrants from other cultures continually adds new members who have grown up under different value systems.

For example, Greek immigrants to the United States would bring the values of Greek society with them.

Each culture is made up of many small groups, and these subgroups may have some norms, customs, beliefs, and values that are different from those held by the larger culture. Country families have customs different from those of city families. Different religious groups have different customs and bring up their children in different ways. When *Psychology Today* magazine asked its readers to answer a questionnaire on death, they found that a Roman Catholic, Protestant, or Jewish background appears to have strong — and different — effects on a person's belief in a life after death and on whether he wants to have his body buried, cremated, or donated to science.

In American cities, persons who belong to the same race or ethnic group tend to live in the same area. When such a group develops its own neighborhood, it also develops its own norms. Going from one ethnic neighborhood to another in New York City is like going from Italy to Poland or from Greece to Puerto Rico. Some minority members live in these ethnic areas because they choose to. Others live there because society applies pressures that keep them there.

One's education, wealth, or job puts him into a subgroup within the culture called a social class. Nearly all societies have classes, but they vary greatly in the ease with which a member of the society can move from one class to another. While the United States has no sharp divisions between social classes, the classes do exist. Most social scientists divide American society into five or six classes, and each class affects its members' beliefs, values, and habits. The beliefs and values of a doctor, for example, are not the same as those of a truck driver, and the beliefs and values of a priest are likely to be different from those of a longshoreman.

One U.S. subculture that concerns psychologists and other social scientists is the subculture of poverty — the lowest part of the lower class. Living in the slums of a big city or in Appalachia or on a poor Indian reservation is not just a matter of money. The constant struggle to live affects the struggler's attitudes and beliefs.

A person who belongs to the subculture of poverty tends to distrust the government and hate the police. His only contact with the governing society is through welfare agencies, doctors in clinics, policemen, and the army. He lives on the brink of financial disaster, is often out of work, and has little hope that he can ever move out of his poverty. Because he lacks hope, he is likely to live on a day-to-day basis and be unable to plan for the future. More and more social scientists are working to find ways to help people break out of this subculture.

All cultures change. Some change slowly, over centuries, and others change rapidly. Members of the culture develop new ways of behaving; they create new products; they make discoveries that change their society; they meet members of other societies with different patterns of behavior. A single change can set off a chain reaction that transforms other aspects of the culture.

When the Portuguese gave steel axes and knives to the Mundurucú Indians of Brazil, they did not realize how their gift would change this Indian society. Steel axes and knives meant that the Mundurucú could clear more jungle and grow more crops than they had in the past. Because contact with the Portuguese and Brazilians opened a market for Mundurucú crops, the Indians continued to increase their farming.

Mundurucú women cultivated manioc and made it into flour. When the flour became a source of wealth, the economic value of women suddenly increased. Fathers became unwilling to part with their now-valuable daughters. When anthropologists Robert and Yolanda Murphy studied the Mundurucú Indians, they found that Mundurucú patterns of living had changed. A woman no longer went to live with her husband's family. Instead, she remained at her home with her mother and sisters and nieces and small nephews. Her husband lived in a dormitory with the other husbands and the unmarried men of the tribe. The new arrangement appeared to work well, but the new society would have looked strange and unnatural to a Mundurucú of 1700.

Mass production of the automobile changed American society. Consider how different your own life would be if you could travel only by horse, by streetcar, or by foot. The automobile made Americans into a nation of travelers, able to go many miles to work or to school. It caused the development of suburbs. It created the highway industry and developed the market for oil and gasoline. When nearly every person had his or her own car — or cars — streetcar and bus service became unprofitable. Automobile exhaust polluted the fresh air of our cities. Car accidents killed thousands of Americans each year. The car changed American society as much as the steel ax changed the life of the Mundurucú.

When a culture is changing rapidly, a generation gap is likely to develop. The older generation clings to the old ideas, beliefs, and attitudes, while the young adopt the new values of the culture. As technology continues to affect U.S. life, our society continues to change rapidly. Young people today are growing up in a world very different from the one their parents knew. Perhaps the uncertainties of life in a changing culture will give us the incentive to develop new ways of coping with the problems of our society.

As we move away from the subject of culture and begin to look at the way an individual perceives his world and reacts to it, little of the reported work by psychologists will refer to the influence of society on a person. But it is important to keep in mind how a culture's ways of behaving and thinking affect the individual the psychologist studies.

Motivation

3

WHEN WE TALK about motivation, we get to the basic *why* in psychology: Why do people act the way they do?

Psychologists use the word *motivation* to say that special conditions cause a person to do something he would not have done without the presence of those conditions. When you walk into a cold room, you turn up the thermostat. If the room had not been cold (special condition), you would not have turned up the heat (act). The cold motivated you to behave so that you would be warm and comfortable again.

People and animals have reasons for most of their behavior, and if we look at the reasons, we find that they have something to do with pleasantness or unpleasantness. A baby cries because he is wet and has learned that crying brings Mother, who changes wet diapers to dry ones. Your dog trots over and lays his head in your lap. If you don't pet him, he pushes his head under your hand until you do. Last month you worked for days building the model of a sailing ship that now gathers dust on a closet shelf.

The baby, the dog, and you all had reasons for your behavior, and these reasons are *motives*. We can call a motive the expectancy of pleasantness or unpleasantness. When events around us cause us to expect something good or bad, that expectation leads us to act.

Earlier we learned that psychologists cannot watch or measure all human behavior. Only the individual who expects the pleasantness or unpleasantness knows exactly how he feels. The psychologist must infer motives from a person's behavior. The psychologist can watch someone striving to get the object that he thinks will bring him pleasure. Just as the finish line in a 100-yard dash is the goal of the runner, so whatever a person wants is his *goal* or *incentive*.

Psychologists watch three features of our behavior to detect the strength of our motives. The *vigor* with which we act is one clue. If you expect a history test in your first class of the day, you probably will walk up the front steps of the school very slowly — you may even be late. But if you are planning to play baseball after school, you probably will run down the steps when class is dismissed.

A second clue lies in how the *direction* of our behavior changes under the same conditions. Every day you walk home after school. If your family is planning to leave on a camping trip right after school on Friday, you will go straight home. On the other hand, if you expect to practice the saxophone for an hour as soon as you get home, you may first stop at the library or get a coke or go over to a friend's house.

Persistence in behavior is the psychologist's third clue. Suppose your teacher recommends a book that will help you to understand the causes of the Civil War. You ask the librarian for the book, and she tells you that someone has checked it out. You forget about the book and never ask for it again. Now suppose that all your friends are talking about *Island of the Blue Dolphins*. Three of them tell you that they could not put down this story of the Indian girl who lived alone on an island for eighteen years. The librarian tells you that the book is out, but this time you do not forget. You ask again and again, until at last you get the book.

Sometimes our motives are triggered by the needs of our bodies. In order to stay alive, we must have air to breathe, food to eat, water to drink, and a temperature that is neither too hot nor too cold.

If you were to spend the day under the blazing desert sun without clothes or hat, you would die. If you stayed all day in the snow without clothing, you would also die. Your body thermostat is set at 98.6° Fahrenheit. When your temperature drops below or climbs above 98.6°, your body goes into immediate action to return your temperature to normal.

When the temperature rises and you become hot, certain nerve cells in the lower part of your brain begin to fire rapidly. You sweat. Your blood vessels expand. Your kidneys reabsorb water. When the temperature drops and you become cold, other nerve cells in the same area of your brain go into action. Their signals make you shiver. Your blood vessels constrict, your thyroid gland works harder so that you burn fuel faster. As soon as your temperature gets back to 98.6°, your systems return to normal.

Your body also has mechanisms that react to lack of food or water or air. All these mechanisms work to keep your body in the normal and healthy state called *homeostasis*.

Your reactions to temperature changes go beyond shivering and sweating and changes in your blood vessels, kidneys, and thyroid. Changes in your body also put you in an *aroused* state. When you are aroused by physiological changes, you feel uncomfortable.

Suppose the temperature climbs to 112°. You begin to sweat and you feel hot. Your body's demand upon you for a cooler temperature is called a *drive*. When this drive arouses you, you are likely to act, and your discomfort gives you a motive. You take off your shirt. You turn on the air conditioner. You drink ice water. You seek the shade if you are outside. You act in ways that you expect will make you feel comfortable.

Hunger is another homeostatic drive. When we feel hungry, we look for food. But something inside our bodies must tell us that we need to eat. Physiologist Walter B. Cannon guessed, as you or I might, that our hunger signals come from our stomachs. He asked subjects to swallow balloons. Then he inflated the balloons and attached them to a mechanism that recorded changes in air pressure. Each time the stomach contracted, it pushed against the full balloon, and the air trapped inside the balloon set the pens of the recorder swinging. He also asked each person to press a device like a telegrapher's key whenever he felt hungry. Cannon was not surprised to find that the subject usually pressed the key at the same time his stomach contracted.

But the solution was not that simple. A psychiatrist — a medical doctor who specializes in mental disorders — tried the same experiment with 74 persons. There was one major difference in Albert Stunkard's experiment, however. Half of his subjects were normal, and the other half were very fat. Sure enough, the normal subjects reported feeling hungry when their stomachs contracted and not feeling hungry when their stomachs were still. But Stunkard could find no relationship between hunger and stomach contractions in fat people. Sometimes they pressed the key when their stomachs contracted, but just as often they pressed the key when their stomachs were still. And we know that when surgeons remove people's stomachs, the patients still feel hungry when they recover.

Researchers who work with animals have found that the brain has a lot to do with the hunger drive. They discovered that if one portion of a rat's *hypothalamus* — which is located in the brainstem — is removed, the rat will stop eating. To keep him alive, researchers must feed him artificially. If another part of the hypothalamus is removed, the rat will grow very fat. This fat rat does not eat constantly, he just eats longer than normal rats do. It is as though a signal that should have told him, "All right, you've had enough to eat," hasn't gotten through. These very fat rats are also gourmets — they eat more of tasty food than their fellow rats, but they eat less if the food tastes bad. The fat rats also refuse to work hard for their food. They don't like to press bars to get their dinners, nor are they willing to take slight electric shocks to get to food.

These rats probably grow so fat because the surgery on their brains upsets their bodies' regulating systems. Apparently the hypothalamus controls the appetite, probably by sending chemicals through the blood stream.

But what about fat people? Tumors that damage the hypothalamus can make people overeat, but such tumors are extremely rare. Psychologist Stanley Schachter looked at all the experiments that had been done with animals and all the experiments that had been done with people, did some more experiments himself, and came up with an answer. Fat people are people who have learned to associate eating with events in the world around them. They eat whenever the clock says it is time to eat or whenever others are eating or whenever they see or smell or are reminded of food.

In one of his experiments, Schachter asked his subjects to taste several kinds of ice cream and decide which was best. He told them to eat as little or as much from each bowl as they needed to judge the quality of the ice cream. One bowl of ice cream was flavored with quinine and was bitter. It tasted awful. Another bowl was full of the richest, creamiest, most delicious ice cream Schachter could find.

The normal subjects ate the same amount of ice cream from each bowl — about a spoonful. But the fat subjects behaved just like the fat rats that would eat only good food. They barely tasted the bitter ice cream, but they ate spoonful after spoonful of the best ice cream.

Studies at St. Luke's Hospital in New York City back up Schachter's theory. Researchers there let people eat as much as they wanted — but the only food they got was a liquid formula very much like vanilla Metrecal. This uninteresting liquid was available at all times. If a person wanted to drink it constantly, he could. All he had to do was to pour it into his glass or push a little button. Every normal subject in the study drank as much formula as he needed to equal the amount of food he usually ate. They neither gained nor lost weight. But the fat subjects all behaved differently. Their food intake dropped dramatically and they began to lose weight. One subject who stayed in the hospital for eight months went from 410 pounds to 190 pounds.

This explains why fat persons find it so hard to lose weight. They have learned to depend on the cues in their environment instead of on the signals inside their bodies to trigger their hunger drives. If a fat person walks by a candy-store window heaped with chocolates, or smells the sizzling meat of a hamburger stand, or goes to a party where bowls of salted nuts and potato chips and dips stand on every table, or picks up a magizine filled with colored pictures of food, or even sees a clock that says "dinnertime," he is lost. He will probably eat even if he has just finished a meal, and if the food before him is good, he will probably eat a lot. In order to lose weight easily, a fat person must either be shut away from the outside world or else fed only food from the kitchen of a very bad cook.

Hunger is not just a single drive. Sometimes you get hungry for a hamburger and french fries or for a platter of spaghetti, and you know that you would not even taste a tuna sandwich or a bowl of oatmeal. When researchers put rats on diets without salt or sugar or fat or calcium or phosphorus or B vitamins — and keep them there for some time — the rats show a strong preference for food that contains the substances their bodies now lack. Sometimes children who need calcium begin to eat plaster from the walls.

But social customs and training can interfere with our natural tendencies to select the kind and amount of food we need to stay healthy. Beriberi — a disease caused by lack of vitamin B_1 — is common in Asia, because polished rice is a major part of the diet and polishing the rice removes the vitamin B_1. We can decide that we hate a certain class of food — vegetables, for example — and shun them until we become undernourished. We can also develop a sweet tooth and eat so much candy that we don't eat enough of the foods we need. This is what happens to the alcoholic, who usually is undernourished because his drinking interferes with his eating — he gets energy from his alcohol but no protein, no vitamins, no minerals.

Hunger is not our only homeostatic drive. Thirst, pain, and the need for oxygen are all important to the survival of animals and people. Pain differs from the other drives we have talked about, because we move away from the source of pain, while at other times we move toward a goal. Because we try to escape from whatever causes us pain, pain is called an *avoidance* drive or an *aversive* drive. We expect situations that brought us pain in the past to be unpleasant and so we avoid them. A child deliberately puts its hand on a hot stove only once.

Sex is a powerful motive in man and in animals, but it is not a homeostatic drive. While sex is necessary if the species is to survive, it is not necessary to the life of the individual. In lower animals, sexual behavior is controlled by hormones and by the lower, more primitive areas of the brain. In higher animals and in man, the higher centers of the brain and learning play a major role.

When any homeostatic drive is out of balance, a person acts in two ways: his body responds automatically and he responds with learned behavior — such as drinking, eating, or turning up the heat — to help his body return to its normal state. Not all motives work to keep our bodies in balance, however. If this were true, once our systems reached a state of balance, we would sit around like happy vegetables until we grew hot or cold, hungry or thirsty, or until the air grew bad or someone threw a rock at us.

At McGill University in Canada, some psychologists decided to find out what would happen if we did reach that state of balance and no stimulation disturbed it. In these experiments, students lay on comfortable beds in rooms by themselves. They wore goggles over their eyes so they could see nothing and padding over their arms and hands so they could touch nothing. Earphones delivered a steady buzz to their ears.

Psychologist W. H. Heron then sat back and waited. His subjects were in a state of *sensory deprivation:* their senses delivered no ordinary stimulation to their brains. Except for an hour or two each day, when the students got up to eat or to go to the toilet, they were to be happy, balanced vegetables. Only they weren't happy.

Afterward, they said that they became restless and unable to think clearly. They could not even daydream. Many dropped out of the experiment. Those who stayed began to have hallucinations. One student felt that he had two bodies, another that his head was detached from his neck, another that his mind was floating in the air above his body. Many students reported seeing visions as complicated as a motion picture. Apparently the brain needs some sort of stimulation to be able to function normally.

People and animals seek stimulation just as they look for food when they are hungry. Curiosity, which is a powerful motive, is closely linked to this need for stimulus change. Many years ago, Charles Darwin watched curious monkeys in an English zoo. A paper bag lay on the floor of their cage. Inside the bag was a live snake. One after another, the monkeys would come over to the bag, cock their heads, take a quick peek into the bag, and back off. In spite of their fear of snakes, the monkeys could not resist looking at the snake in the bag.

Monkeys are not the only curious animals. Stephen Glickman spent five years testing the curiosity of the animals in Chicago's Lincoln Park Zoo. He tested more than 300 animals by putting objects like wooden blocks and rods, steel chains, rubber tubes, and pieces of paper into their cages. None of these objects was frightening, but all were strange to the animals. When they first saw the objects, most animals sniffed or bit at them, pushed them around, or carried them about. Apes, monkeys, raccoons, cougars, lions, tigers, leopards, jaguars, and foxes turned out to be very curious animals.

One crocodile acted just like an ape or a tiger. He carried each object into the water, nudged it with his snout, bit it, and shook it in his jaws. He turned out to be an exceptional reptile. Other crocodiles, alligators, lizards, and snakes ignored the objects in their cages.

Generally, the more highly developed an animal is, the more curious it turns out to be. But animals that must kill to eat are more curious than animals that are eaten. This turns out to be good sense for the survival of the species. If you are the kind of animal that is another animal's favorite dinner, you will live longer if you don't explore strange objects and strange places. Glickman placed a group of mice in a cage that let the mice go into a room where an owl lived. The mice that had been the most curious in earlier experiments were the mice that visited the owl's room and were, therefore, the mice that became the owl's dinner.

We find it easy to understand the monkey that works for an hour to open a window latch so he can look at the world outside, but harder to understand the monkey that works just as intently to open and close locks that lead to nothing. The monkey that manipulates the locks solely for the fun of opening and closing them is behaving very much like the person who spends hours manipulating a puzzle such as the colored cubes of Instant Insanity, or the pieces of wood that can — with care — be assembled into a cube, or the numbered pieces of plastic that can be moved inside a frame until they fall into correct order. The reward comes from the satisfaction of solving the puzzle, and the simple latch may be just as perplexing a problem to the monkey as the colored cubes are to you.

Another motive that helps direct behavior is our need to have our world behave in harmonious ways. Of course, it would disturb us if rain began to fall up instead of down, or if we suddenly started to float in the air. We need the stability of a consistent world, in which things behave as we expect them to. Our demand for consistency goes far beyond the rules of the physical world; we also demand consistency between our beliefs and our actions. When we find that our beliefs and actions do not match, we are uncomfortable. In order to get out of this unpleasant state, we may even change what we believe so that our actions will not make us unhappy.

Studies show that the more cigarettes a person smokes, the less likely he is to believe that smoking causes cancer. The smoker has two bits of information that do not match: "I smoke and I do not want to develop cancer," and "Smoking causes cancer." He can stop smoking and solve his problem, or he can change his beliefs so that he can continue to smoke. There are many ways to alter the knowledge that smoking causes cancer. The smoker may say, "All my friends smoke and they don't have cancer," or "It takes years to develop cancer, and I can stop before the disease appears," or "I'd rather smoke and live a short life than live a long one without the pleasures of smoking," or "Not everybody who smokes gets cancer." The smoker searches for a solution that appears logical, even though his answer makes no sense to a non-smoker.

Psychologists first recognized our need to organize the world when they studied a religious group that believed the world was coming to an end on a particular date. When the date came and passed, the members of the group acted in different ways. Those who were only half-hearted members decided the group was wrong. But members who truly believed — those who had sold all their possessions or who had given interviews to the press — refused to give up the belief. They said that the date had only been postponed, or that God had cancelled the destruction of the world because they had believed so strongly, or that the world would indeed end soon but they had picked the wrong date.

From this study Leon Festinger developed the idea of *cog-*

nitive dissonance (which literally means lack of mental harmony). Festinger saw that if a person has two inconsistent ideas, beliefs, or opinions, he is thrown into the unpleasant state Festinger called cognitive dissonance. He can get out of that state only by changing one of the ideas. The true believers could not change the fact that the world still existed, but — just like the smoker — they changed other beliefs so they could keep their original faith.

Our society puts a great value on doing things well and getting ahead. People who succeed by this standard are those with a strong need for achievement. They learn fastest and work best not to get money, but simply to do a better job than others. They expect pleasure — and get it — from doing things well. Many of us have a need for achievement. If that need is strong throughout a society, says psychologist David McClelland, the society is likely to grow in wealth and power. He believes this so strongly that he has been developing ways to raise a person's need for achievement.

A psychologist can determine this need in you by handing you a group of pictures. You look at the pictures and then tell him a story about each scene you see. McClelland, who devised this way to measure the need for achievement, would ask you to tell him what is happening in the picture, what happened before the scene you are looking at, what the people are thinking about, what each of them wants, and what will happen later. If you have a strong need for achievement, you will reveal it by the story you tell.

People who show a high need on this test are also likely to doodle in distinctive ways. They fill a page with doodles, instead of leaving the bottom of the page blank; they draw many S-shaped and diagonal lines; they draw circles, rectangles, stars, and triangles; and they draw lots of parallel lines that are not attached to other lines. Persons with a low need for achievement draw wavy, connected lines, blotchy lines, and often doodle over their doodles.

Psychologist Evan Davies looked at the pottery of ancient Crete and discovered that the decorations told the story of Crete's history. When the Minoan civilization of Crete was growing and powerful, the designs on the pottery looked like doodles drawn by someone with a high need for achievement: lots of S-shaped or diagonal lines appeared on each piece. But as the Minoan civilization weakened, their pottery decorations resembled the doodles of a person with a low need for achievement.

All of us need love, and few would deny that love is a basic motive of man. It turns out that love is just as important to a small monkey as it is to me or to you. Psychologists Harry and Margaret Harlow took baby monkeys away from their mothers when they were less than a day old. The babies were given two adopted mothers: one mother was made of wire mesh and the other was made of wood covered with soft terry cloth. Half the baby monkeys got their milk from a nipple attached to the wire mother and the other half got their milk from the cloth mother.

All the little monkeys spent hours every day clinging to the soft, terry cloth mother. Even babies that got their milk from the wire mother cuddled against the cloth mother. If anything strange or frightening disturbed the little monkeys, they ran to the cloth mother and clung to her.

Apparently, the baby monkey's love for its mother does not depend on food. The warmth and cuddliness that come from contact with another are important sources of pleasure. The Harlows called this *contact comfort* and pointed out that such contact is necessary for the development of love.

When these little monkeys grew up, they could not get along with other monkeys, and most of them had no interest in the opposite sex. When some of the female monkeys did mate and have babies, they were bad mothers. They pushed their babies away and beat them so savagely that the Harlows had to take the babies away from them.

Human babies share the little monkeys' need for contact comfort. Psychiatrist René Spitz became concerned about the high death rate among babies in orphan homes. When he investigated, he discovered that the babies were left alone in their cribs all day. They were touched only when they needed food or changing. Spitz found that picking up and cuddling these babies could cut the death rate and help the babies to develop into normal children.

People need people. We generally expect pleasure from the company of others and feel lonely if we unexpectedly find ourselves alone. Suppose you have planned to study after school. When you get home, you find a note that tells you your parents were called away and won't be home until after dinner. You walk through the house, which suddenly seems large and empty. You sit down at your desk and try to study but find you are just staring at the print. You had planned to be alone in your room, but you hadn't planned to be alone in the house. You are lonely. Psychologists call this need to be with others the need for *affiliation*.

If you are the oldest child in your family, the chances are that you would feel lonelier in that empty house than a younger brother or sister would. Some studies show that first-born children have a stronger affiliation motive than later-born children. When they are anxious, first-borns turn to other people. This has a curious effect in later life. When first-borns have severe personal problems, they are likely to go to a psychologist or psychiatrist for help. When later-borns have severe problems, they may drink instead. Alcoholics are likely to have older brothers or sisters.

Stanley Schachter, who has studied the affiliation motive, believes that first-borns turn to people because their parents were unsure of themselves. When their first baby cried or fretted, they ran to it, and the baby learned that people take care of one's problems. When their second and third babies came along, the parents were sure of themselves. They were not so likely to worry about a fretting baby, and later the baby was not so likely to depend upon people when he got into trouble.

Some of our motives are stronger than others. Abraham Maslow ranked our motives and said that a man is not free to develop himself fully and to respond to the motives at the top of the list until his lower motives have been satisfied. For example, a man who is hungry and must spend all his time searching for food is not likely to sit under a tree and contemplate the beauties of nature. Nor is he likely to paint a beautiful picture or write a great novel or poem. Homeostatic drives are basic, and we must satisfy them first. Once we no longer worry about food, water, and shelter from the elements, other motives can take over. We begin to think about love and acceptance; we strive to succeed at some task.

But Maslow believed that there is yet another group of motives. When we feel loved and accepted, when we respect ourselves and feel that others respect us, we begin to respond to a different kind of motive. Maslow called these new motives *metaneeds*. Metaneeds include justice, goodness, unity, beauty and order. Only under their influence, said Maslow, can we develop our full talents and potentials.

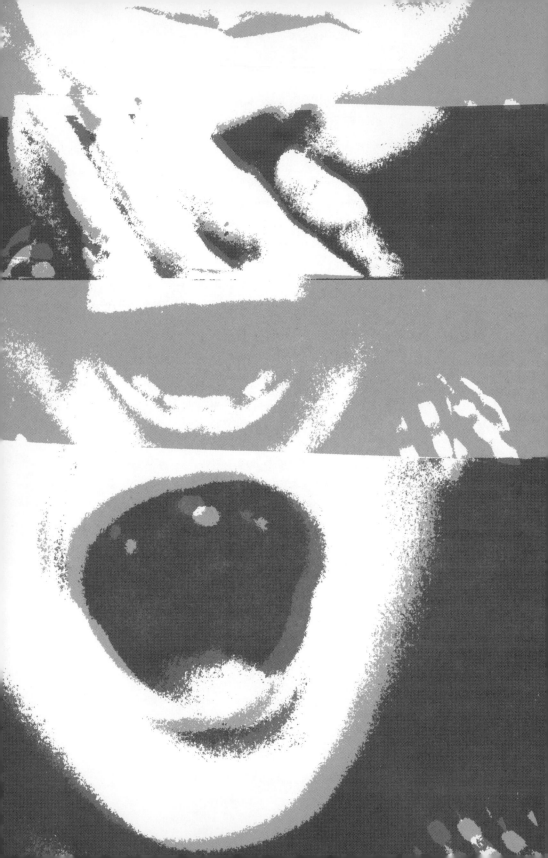

Emotions

4

No ONE NEEDS to tell you that emotions are powerful or that they can disrupt your behavior. They can also save your life. When your emotions come to life suddenly and strongly, all sorts of changes are going on inside your body. Your body is preparing for emergency action: for fight, flight, or fright.

Psychologists cannot see your emotions, but they can see or measure some of the changes that are going on inside your body. Your heart beats faster, your blood pressure goes up, the pupils of your eyes grow larger, you sweat, your breathing changes, your mouth gets dry, your skin conducts more electricity, your muscles may shake, you get gooseflesh, and your hair stands on end. With very strong emotion, you may get dizzy or sick at your stomach or even lose control of your bladder or bowels.

When these changes come about, your adrenal glands are pouring adrenalin into your blood stream. Adrenalin (called epinephrine by researchers) stimulates the nerve cells so that proper signals can cross the gaps between them. It is this product of your adrenal glands that keeps your heart pounding and hands trembling long after the emergency has passed.

Most soldiers are afraid during battle but continue to fight. During World War II, L. F. Schaffer asked 4500 air-force pilots, navigators, bombadiers, and gunners how they felt during combat missions. Most of them said they were afraid: 86 percent told Schaffer that their hearts pounded and their pulses beat rapidly; 80 percent had dry mouths and throats; 79 percent broke out in a cold sweat; 76 percent had butterflies in their stomachs; 65 percent had to go the bathroom often; 64 percent found themselves trembling; and 38 percent became sick at their stomachs. The normal reaction to fear is to run, but these men kept on flying their missions. It may be that having a job to perform helps us to control fear.

The lie detector takes advantage of these physical changes to detect the emotion of guilt. The lie detector assumes that a person who lies cannot keep his adrenal glands, his heart, his blood pressure and his skin from responding — no matter how controlled and calm he may appear. But the machine's recordings are very difficult to interpret, and it takes great skill and care to prepare and ask the questions so that the results will be accurate. If a person is so frightened or upset that he reacts emotionally to all questions, the test will reveal nothing. On the other hand, a person who has learned to control his internal organs — which is difficult but not impossible — can spoil the test. For these reasons, results of lie detector tests are rarely used in the courtroom.

When a baby is born, it cannot feel joy or anger or love or fear. K. M. Bridges studied 112 babies from the time they were born until they were two years old. She describes a new-born baby's emotion as excitement — a generally upleasant reaction. By the time a baby is three months old, it can tell the difference between distress and excitement, and it has learned delight — a pleasant emotion. By the time a baby is six months old, it feels fear, disgust, and anger. And by the time a child is two years old, it knows most other emotions: jealousy, joy, elation, and affection.

Our emotions strongly influence our motives. Our motives lead us to move toward a goal or away from something. As we get closer to our goal — or drop farther from it — we feel joy or elation or fear or anger or disgust, and these feelings strengthen our motives.

More research has been done on fear and on anger than on other emotions. They are easier to study in the laboratory than the pleasanter emotions, because it is easier to detect them in an animal or a person. And it is important for us to understand them. Fear or anger can make us do things we may be sorry for later. Perfect understanding of these emotions might help us to get rid of violence, wars, and emotional disturbances.

We feel angry when we want something and can't have it. A baby held so tightly that it cannot move will turn red, squirm, and cry. A child told that it cannot go to the circus may kick and scream and hold its breath. An adult may curse if a sudden rainstorm cancels a golf date.

Psychologists say these persons are *frustrated*. The strength of their anger depends upon two things: how much they wanted to reach their goals and how sure they were that they would reach them. If the child secretly thought that his parents would not take him to the circus, he might only pout. But if his father had promised to take him, he would be likely to throw a temper tantrum. If the adult had planned a social game of golf, he might be only annoyed, but if a big business deal depended on the game, he might become furious.

Animals and people often respond to frustration and anger by attacking. Such attacks on a person or an object are called *aggression*. Aggression may be by word or deed. Fighting and name-calling are both examples of aggression. The person or object attacked may have no connection with whatever caused the anger. A girl may hit her brother after she has been scolded. A man who has been refused a raise may come home and start an argument with his wife. A pigeon that fails to get the grain it expects will attack another pigeon, or even a stuffed one.

Three psychologists who wanted to see how people react to frustration kept a group of college students awake all night. R. R. Sears, C. I. Hovland and Neal Miller pretended that they were conducting an experiment on the effects of extreme tiredness. They did everything they could to frustrate the students. They would not let the students smoke or talk, and promised games and food that never showed up. The students wanted to sleep but could not. Everything they asked for was refused. Thereupon students began making nasty remarks about the experiment and the psychologists, and asked if the psychologists were crazy. One student drew a picture of injured and bleeding bodies. He said it was a picture of psychologists.

For a long time, most psychologists believed that frustration built up inside a person, like steam in a boiler, and that if it had no way to escape, the frustration would eventually explode in aggression. People who believed that frustration almost always led to aggression said that we should all take part in competitive sports or go to football games or watch violent plays or violent movies in order to release our hostile feelings in harmless ways.

Most people, including some psychologists, still accept this theory. When you excuse a person's bad behavior with the words, "He's just letting off steam," you are stating that theory. Today other psychologists believe that frustration does not have to lead to aggression, and that playing or watching competitive sports and viewing violent dramas make us more rather than less aggressive.

Psychologists like Albert Bandura of Stanford University noticed that frustration does not always produce violence. Bandura points out that while some people whose goals are blocked become aggressive, others try harder, or ask for help, or else they just give up or turn to alcohol or other drugs. He believes that the way we respond to frustration depends upon the way we have learned to respond.

Our parents, our friends, our teachers, and our books, magazines, movies, and television teach us to "stand up" for ourselves. They let us know that we can get what we want by aggressive words or actions. Sometimes we learn aggression when our parents think they are teaching us the opposite. If your father beats you for fighting, you may stop punching your friends, but you will probably decide that violence works just fine. It stopped you from fighting.

Not even animals that we consider aggressive are naturally violent. For example, we expect cats to kill rats. Watching a kitten pounce upon a mouse, we might even say that a cat is a natural killer. But for more than forty years we have known that kittens must learn to kill rats.

K. Y. Kuo conducted a carefully controlled experiment with a group of kittens. He raised one group of kittens by themselves. Another group of kittens grew up with their rat-killing mothers. A third group grew up with rat companions. Half the kittens in each group never ate a bite of meat. The other half had a normal cat's diet, full of fish and meat.

Almost all the kittens who lived with their rat-killing mothers became great killers of rats. A diet without meat had only one effect: the vegetarian kittens killed rats but didn't eat them. Just under half of the kittens that grew up alone killed rats. Kittens that grew up with rat friends refused to kill rats — even when they were hungry.

Now Kuo decided to see if any of these peace-loving kittens would learn to kill rats. He put them where they could watch other cats kill rats. After their lessons, 82 percent of the peaceful kittens that had grown up alone became rat-killers, but only 7 percent of the kittens who had learned to love rats ever killed one.

Frustration is not the only thing that makes animals aggressive. Nathan Azrin has shown that animals react to pain by attacking. When he put pairs of rats, mice, hamsters, raccoons, foxes, cats, turtles, squirrels, monkeys, alligators, or snakes in cages and ran electricity through the cage floor, the animals almost always attacked each other.

Each kind of animal attacked in its own way: the monkeys used their hands, the snakes hissed, the raccoons used their forepaws — but they all bit. A shocked animal would attack a different kind of animal — one it normally feared and ran from. A shocked animal would even attack a stuffed toy.

Psychologists call pain an avoidance drive and say that we move away from the source of pain. Azrin thought about this and changed the experiment so that monkeys could either attack a stuffed toy or push a lever that would stop the shock. The monkeys chose to push the lever, and attacked only when they could not escape the painful electricity.

Not all animals attacked when shocked. Azrin found that skunks, iguanas, tarantulas, and chickens failed to attack. But anyone who has ever kicked a footstool that he tripped over in the dark might guess that a man can respond to pain just as a rat does.

When we are afraid, we expect something unpleasant to happen: we expect to be hurt, to be alone, to fail a test. And it is easy for us to learn fear. More than fifty years ago, J. B. Watson, one of the early American psychologists, taught a little boy to fear anything that was white and fuzzy. Watson showed Albert, who was nine months old, a tame white rat. Albert was not afraid and seemed curious about the rat. Then, whenever Watson showed Albert the rat, someone made a loud noise just behind Albert's head. The noise frightened Albert and made him cry. Soon Albert cried every time he saw the white rat — or even a white, fuzzy stuffed toy.

The feeling of fear is extremely unpleasant. Anything that will reduce that feeling or make it go away becomes a goal. Albert avoided the white rat because the rat became the signal that he would hear a loud, unpleasant and frightening noise.

When Neal Miller studied fear in animals, he found that frightened rats behave very much like frightened babies. Miller used a cage with two compartments, one painted white and one painted black. When the rats were in the white section of the cage, Miller gave them electric shocks through the wire floor. The rats showed all the signs of rat fear: they became tense, they crouched, and they lost control of their bladders and bowels. Before long just putting them into the white compartment made them react with fear.

Then Miller fixed the door between the two compartments so that it could be opened by turning a wheel. The rats quickly learned to turn the wheel. As soon as they found themselves in the white compartment, they would race over, open the door, and dash into the black section of the cage. The rats that got the strongest shocks learned to open the door first.

The white compartment became a signal that a painful shock was on its way, and the rats learned to get out in order to avoid the shock.

When we are afraid, whatever we do that lets us escape

from our fear will be the thing we do the next time we are afraid. Albert cried when he saw the white rat. He was picked up, so he cried again the next time he saw the rat.

Our responses to fear can be helpful or harmful. Suppose you have a history test tomorrow, and when you open your book to study, you find that you are frightened. You haven't studied much lately, and Ms. Jefferson's tests are always difficult, made up so that you can't bluff your way through them. You can keep on studying and learn to master your fear by facing it, or you can close your book and go to the movies. At the theater you'll forget about the test and your fears — and you'll do poorly in tomorrow's examination. Because you escaped from your fear by going to the movies, the chances are high that the next time you face a test, you'll go to the movies again — just as those rats scampered into the black side of the cage. Your goal has changed from passing the test to avoiding your fear.

Once a person or an animal becomes afraid of something, it is very hard to get rid of the fear. When Miller stopped running electricity through the floor of the white compartment, the rats still ran into the black compartment every time. They never stayed in the white section long enough to find out if they would be shocked. Suppose that when you were only two, you fell into deep water and nearly drowned. You became so frightened of water that, just as the rat avoided the white compartment, you made up excuses to stay away from swimming pools and lakes and rivers and oceans. As long as you avoid every chance to find out that water need not harm you, you will probably keep your fear of water.

Sometimes we are afraid and don't know why. No one is threatening to hurt us, we're not alone, and we don't expect to fail at anything. But our distress will not go away. Psychologists call this kind of fear *anxiety*, and sometimes we need the help of psychologists to get over it.

We learn to show our emotions in ways that our society finds suitable. Our culture teaches us to express our emotions at the right time, in the right place, and in the right way. A tiny child may scream and stamp his foot when he is angry, but he soon learns from his family, his teachers, and his friends that such behavior is not permitted.

Different cultures allow their members to show their emotions in different ways. In China, a person opens his eyes wide when he is angry, sticks out his tongue when he is surprised, claps his hands when he is disappointed, and scratches his ears and cheeks when he is happy. In Japan, an embarrassed man does not blush, he smiles. In Italy, a man is expected to cry or to show his temper at times when English and American men have learned to show no emotion.

It seems that psychologists should be able to tell what emotion a person is feeling, but — except in cases of extreme and overpowering emotion — it is difficult. Our own culture frowns on most emotional displays, and we learn to mask our feelings.

When people look at photographs of faces expressing different emotions, often they cannot agree on what emotion they are seeing. They find it easier to agree if the picture has been posed by an actor.

Skilled actors communicate emotions without using a single word; they make conscious attempts to show emotions in their faces and in the ways they hold their bodies, and they are helped by the circumstances of the story they are acting out. The spectator knows from the plot what emotion he would feel in the actor's place, and so he correctly interprets the actor's slumped shoulders and bowed head as grief or depression or deep thought — depending upon the story.

One physiologist, Manfred Clynes, believes that our brains always react in the same way for the same emotion, and that this reaction reaches our muscles. He has been able to show this in the laboratory.

Clynes seated a subject in a straight-backed chair and asked him to rest the middle finger of his right hand on a device that looked much like a telegrapher's key. This key was wired to a machine that measured the finger's downward pressure and its pressure toward or away from the body. Each time a person pressed the key, the machine recorded the pressures and produced two tracings that gave a precise picture of the finger's movement.

Clynes asked his subject to imagine that he felt anger or love or joy or grief or hate or sex or reverence, and to express that emotion with the pressure of his middle finger. Each time a subject imagined a particular emotion, his finger produced the same tracing — and one person's tracing for anger, for example, looked like any other person's anger tracing. What's more, Clynes found that people in Japan or Mexico or Bali produced the same tracings for love or hate or grief that people in this country produced.

Fear is one emotion that defeats this method of detection. It escapes analysis because fear is an avoidance drive and we respond to fear by withdrawing. Whenever Clynes asked a subject to imagine fear, the subject responded by pulling his finger away. There was no pressure on the key. Clynes has never been able to record a tracing for fear.

We can't go around wired to a machine that spells out our emotions for others. In fact, we have enough difficulty deciding on our own emotions. Research has shown that before we can feel an emotion two things must happen. Our bodies must go through the physiological changes that accompany emotion and we must be in a situation that we can label as happy or frightening or sad.

Stanley Schachter and J. E. Singer told a group of students that they would be testing the effects of Suproxin, a new, super vitamin-C compound, on vision. Then they injected half the students with a drug that causes the body changes we associate with strong emotion — rapid heartbeat, increased blood pressure, muscle tremor, and rapid breathing. The rest of the students — the control group — got injections of salt water. (Salt water has no effect on the body.)

After they got their injections, the students were left in a room, while Schachter watched them through a one-way mirror. In the group was a confederate of Schachter's who performed according to a script. In half of the experiments the confederate acted extremely happy: he made paper airplanes and flew them; he performed antics; he set up the wastebasket as a goal and played basketball with pieces of crumpled paper. In the rest of the experiments, the confederate pretended he was angry: he complained about the experiment; he said the questionnaires they were filling out were stupid; he stamped out of the room.

When the stooge pretended to be happy, the students who got the drug acted much happier than the students who got salt water. When the stooge pretended to be angry, the students who got the drug became angrier than those who got salt water. It appeared that once the drug began to work, the students in happy surroundings decided that they must be happy and the students in an angry atmosphere decided that they were angry.

This experiment supports Bandura's theory that we learn aggression. If the same physiological changes cause anger in one situation and happiness in another, we apparently learn to interpret the same body sensations in different ways. This suggests that our aggressive feelings are neither inevitable nor inborn.

Schachter wanted to make sure that his results were correct. With Ladd Wheeler, he next did experiments in a different situation. Again, one group got salt-water injections and a second group got the drug that causes the body changes we associate with emotion. But this time, a third group got a tranquilizer. Schachter placed each student so that he could neither see nor hear his companions and then showed a very funny fifteen-minute sequence from a Jack Carson movie, *The Good Humor Man*.

The researchers watched the students closely during the showing of the movie. Sure enough, the students who got the drug enjoyed the movie more than the others. They laughed out loud and were the only ones who shook with belly laughs. The students who got the salt water seemed to think the movie was funny, but they smiled instead of laughing out loud. The students who got the tranquilizer seemed to enjoy the movie less than the others. Afterward, when the students rated the movie, their ratings matched the ways they had reacted. One student who got the drug said, "I just couldn't understand why I was laughing during the movie. Usually I hate Jack Carson and this kind of nonsense."

Our brains have a lot to do with our emotions and our motives. That same hypothalamus that appears to tell rats when to stop eating can do a lot of other things. If researchers excite one part of the hypothalamus with an electric current, rats that have just been fed will begin to eat again. If they excite another part of the hypothalamus, rats will begin to drink, even if they have just finished drinking. Other researchers have found that electricity in still other parts of the hypothalamus affects rats' sexual behavior or makes them angry or afraid.

James Olds implanted *electrodes* (tiny wires that conduct electricity) into the hypothalamus of rats and placed them where they could press a lever that would send a half-second jolt of electric current through the electrodes and into their brains. He found that if the electrodes were placed in a certain section of the hypothalamus, the rats would press the bar over and over again — sometimes as many as 5000 times in one hour. And they paid no attention to food, to water, or to attractive female rats. Some of them pressed the lever until they collapsed from exhaustion. As soon as they had rested, they went back to the lever and began pressing once again. It appeared that Olds had found a "pleasure-center" in the rat's brain.

Other researchers have found that an electric current in other areas of the hypothalamus is decidedly unpleasant to rats. A shock there will make the rat do whatever he can to escape the current.

José Delgado has used electricity with monkeys, with bulls, and with people. He stepped into a bullring, stood in the path of a charging bull, and pressed a button that sent electricity through the bull's brain. The charging animal stopped in its tracks.

When he sent electric current into the brains of monkeys, Delgado found that a monkey's social position affected the way it responded. Current in one part of a boss monkey's brain usually made him aggressive and likely to attack the other monkeys he ruled. Delgado wondered if he could use electricity to make a timid monkey attack. He sent current to the same place in Lina's brain, but she behaved differently with different monkeys. When she was with monkeys more powerful than she, she hardly ever attacked. But when Delgado put her with monkeys who were equal to her or below her in rank, she attacked often. Monkey society apparently has a powerful influence on monkey aggression. It appears that, even when provoked, a monkey will show no more violence than it knows its companions will put up with.

Less work has been done with human beings, but Delgado has placed electrodes into the brains of patients suffering from epilepsy. Epilepsy is a brain disorder that can be mild or severe. In severe cases, the victim has attacks that can send him into convulsions.

Delgado put electrodes into the brain of a woman whose epilepsy could not be controlled by medicine. These electrodes were not inserted into her hypothalamus, but into her right temporal lobe — which is at the side of the brain but not as deep as the hypothalamus. When electricity passed into her brain, she giggled, said that the left side of her body tingled, and that she enjoyed the feeling. As the current passed through her brain again and again, she began to flirt with her therapist and said that she would like to marry him.

In another study, a man who suffered from narcolepsy (a disorder in which a person suddenly falls into a deep sleep) found that whenever he began to fall asleep, a push on the button that delivered electricity into his brain would wake him up. He also found the electricity very pleasant and sexually stimulating.

After Olds first published his experiments describing the rats that spent their days delivering electricity to their brains, many people became concerned. They had visions of a dictator who bent people to his will by rewarding them with jolts of electricity. There is little basis for these fears. No one has ever changed a person's personality with electricity or made a robot of him. It is true that we can use electricity to make a person more aggressive or more loving, but the way he expresses that emotional impulse depends upon his own experiences over the years.

When you feel hunger or thirst or rage or fear, no one has pushed a button to send electricity into your brain. Something must trigger the impulses from your brain to your heart, your lungs, your stomach, and your adrenal glands. Studies indicate that cells in the central nervous system, called *neurons*, manufacture various chemicals that play different roles in our emotions. These chemicals are called transmitter chemicals because they transmit impulses from one neuron to the next.

Sebastian Grossman implanted tiny stainless steel tubes into the brains of rats. He chose the part of the hypothalamus that controls eating. When he injected norepinephrine, a transmitter chemical, through the tubes, rats that had just finished eating began to eat once more. When he injected acetylcholine, another transmitter, rats began to drink. While his experiments have been difficult to repeat, it may be that both transmitters and electricity stimulate neurons in the same way.

Acetylcholine may do more than make rats drink. When Douglas King and his colleagues at Princeton University injected a drug that acts like acetylcholine into the hypothalamus of a rat, the rat became warlike. Twelve rats that had never before killed mice or seen mice killed became murderers. After one of these rats got an injection, it would grab a mouse and bite through its spinal cord the moment the mouse entered the cage.

When King injected a drug that stops the action of acetylcholine into the brains of killer rats, they stopped killing. They went up to mice, they sniffed them, and sometimes they followed them, but they never attacked. Before they got their injections, these same rats had always killed mice within two minutes after the mice were placed in the cage.

The drug Schachter used in his experiments with students' emotions was epinephrine, that secretion of the adrenal glands that prepares our bodies for emergencies. This drug is associated with fear. Mental patients who are depressed and fearful have more epinephrine in their blood streams than mental patients who are continually angry. White rabbits and domestic animals also have high amounts of epinephrine in their blood streams. Angry mental patients, on the other hand, and wild animals like lions and tigers, show high amounts of norepinephrine — another secretion of the adrenal glands and the same drug that Grossman found would make full rats eat. (Epinephrine and norepinephrine are manufactured in both neurons and adrenal glands.)

This research with chemicals and with the brain shows that the ways in which our bodies work have a great deal to do with our feelings. It works the other way, too. The ways we feel about things that happen to us influence our bodies.

When we find ourselves in situations that keep our adrenal glands pouring adrenalin into our blood streams, our hearts beating faster than usual, and our blood pressures at high levels, we may develop physical illnesses. High blood pressure, skin disease, migraine headaches, asthma, and ulcers can result from emotional problems.

Thomas H. Holmes has found that when a number of unusual events happen to us at about the same time, we are likely to get sick. His studies show that even colds, tuberculosis, and diseases of the large intestine seem to be triggered by changes in a person's life.

The events do not have to be unpleasant. They include marriage, Christmas, vacation, moving, and outstanding personal achievement. But they also include divorce, death of a family member, jail, and losing one's job.

When Steven Bramwell studied 100 college football players, he found that changes in the athletes' lives during the previous year seemed to lead to injuries on the playing field. Ten players were injured more than once during the season; seven of these ten came from Bramwell's "high-risk" group, made up of athletes with many life changes during the past year. Half of the players in the high-risk group were injured at least once during the season; only 10 percent of the players in the low-risk group were injured.

It seems that we get colds and minor illnesses when we go through the minor crises of Christmas, vacation, changes in eating or sleeping habits, or visits from mothers-in-law. When events pile up and we struggle with overwhelming crises, we tend to get more serious illnesses such as tuberculosis or heart disease. Perhaps crises cause us to lose both sleep and appetite, and our lowered resistance leaves us open to infection. Or perhaps the more energy we must spend coping with our environment, the less we have to spend on preventing disease.

Learning

5

LEARNING BRINGS ABOUT a change in a person's or animal's behavior. As the result of experience, a dog learns to sit when he hears a command; a child learns to ride a bicycle; you learn to speak French; your sister in medical school learns to diagnose tuberculosis; your father learns to tune the engine in his car.

When we learn, something happens in our nervous systems. Most psychologists assume that the change is permanent and that it takes place in the neurons. The easiest way to study learning is to watch for changes in behavior, and the easiest place to start is with a simple animal in a laboratory.

About the time this century began, Ivan Pavlov, a Russian physiologist, noticed a strange thing happening in his laboratory. Pavlov was studying dogs, trying to find out just what happened when food passed through a dog's digestive system. He knew that when food was placed in a dog's mouth, its salivary glands began to pour out saliva. To his surprise, he found that when the dogs' keeper walked into the laboratory, the dogs began to drool. Saliva flowed as freely as it did when they had a spoonful of meat powder in their mouths.

Pavlov thought about this and realized that the keeper usually fed the dogs. He guessed that the dogs had connected the keeper with the food. Pavlov set up an experiment. He sounded a tuning fork and then put meat powder in a dog's mouth. At first, saliva appeared only when the powder was in the mouth. But soon, the moment the tuning fork sounded its note, the dog began to drool. Pavlov had *conditioned* the dog to respond to the sound.

Psychologists call this a *conditioned response,* and they call Pavlov's work *classical conditioning.* Classical conditioning is the simplest form of learning — even worms do it. It takes place without any conscious effort by the learner, who usually does not know what is happening.

When John Watson frightened baby Albert with the white rat, he was using classical conditioning. The loud noise just behind Albert's head was the *unconditioned stimulus,* just as the food was the unconditioned stimulus for the dog. The white rat was the *conditioned stimulus* that made Albert respond just as he had responded to the noise. The sound of the tuning fork was the conditioned stimulus for the dog.

Watson was an early psychologist who studied behavior in this simple form. He believed that psychologists should ignore what goes on inside people. He was not interested in his subjects' ideas, opinions, or feelings, only in their actions. Watson believed that all learning is based on classical conditioning. He called his psychology *behaviorism* and he was one of the first *behaviorists.*

Watson made the study of behavior too simple. A very different type of conditioning goes on in laboratories today. It is a more complicated form of learning, but it is easy to study. In *operant conditioning,* the animal must do something to earn its reward. It must press a bar or peck a key or solve a puzzle.

Put a hungry rat into a small box, and it will explore, sniffing the edges and corners, nudging every object in sight. At last, it accidentally pushes a bar and a pellet of food drops into a cup. The rat greedily eats the food and sniffs around for more. Gradually he learns that pressing the bar produces food. A psychologist would say that the food has *reinforced* bar-pressing in the rat — we would say that the food has strengthened the chances that the rat will press the bar again when he is hungry. Because food is very pleasant to a hungry rat, the food is *positive reinforcement*.

Sometimes rats must learn to run through mazes to earn their food. One of the simplest mazes is a box shaped like the letter *T*. The rat runs along a narrow corridor until he comes to a place where he must turn either to the right or to the left. At the end of one passage waits food or water; the other passage is empty. When rats first enter the T-maze, some will turn to the right, others to the left. After several trips along the maze, a rat learns to run straight for the food. In complicated mazes, a rat must make a series of turns like the one in the T-maze.

Teaching a hungry rat to press a bar or to take the correct turn in a winding passageway seems so simple that it is hardly fair to call it learning. But this simple technique of rewarding an animal when it does what you want it to do can produce complicated behavior.

Barnabus, a male rat whose home is a college psychology laboratory, learned to perform a dazzling trick. When a light flashes in his cage, Barnabus scrambles up a circular mesh staircase to a landing. There he dashes across a moat, scampers up a sixteen-step ladder, and — with his teeth and claws — drags a small red car into position. He climbs into the car and pedals to the bottom of another staircase. Barnabus runs up these stairs and squeezes through a long, narrow, glass tube. At the end of the tube is an elevator, and as the elevator slowly descends with its furry passenger, Barnabus pulls on a chain that raises the university flag. The elevator comes to rest at the bottom of his large aluminum and glass cage, and Barnabus presses a bar. The bar makes a buzzer sound, and the sound tells Barnabus that he may eat as much as he likes for one minute.

Barnabus learned to do this complicated trick — which takes him two minutes to perform — one segment at a time. At first he got his food after each bit of behavior in the long chain, but gradually his reinforcement was postponed, so that he had to work harder for each food reward.

Teaching an animal to perform in this way is called *shaping* behavior. The psychologists who trained Barnabus shaped his behavior as if they were sculptors molding clay into a statue. You can train your own dog just as psychologists trained Barnabus or as the trainers at Sea World teach their dolphin actors to perform.

Suppose you want to teach your dog to turn in circles. Obviously, you cannot feed your dog every thirty seconds during the training period. He would have to stop each time to eat, and when his stomach became too full, he would no longer work for the food, which is his *primary reinforcement*.

You need a *secondary reinforcer*. This reinforcer is a signal that comes to stand for the primary reinforcer. Because the two often occur together, the animal — or the person — comes to respond to the secondary reinforcer with all the enthusiasm with which he greeted the primary reinforcer. A baby responds to its mother, who stands for food, dry clothes, and contact comfort. Most persons respond to money, which stands for all the things money can buy.

A sound makes a good secondary reinforcer for dog training. A clicker, like those you use at Hallowe'en, works well. Your first task is to teach your dog to connect the clicker with food. Wait until your dog is hungry. Each time you snap the clicker, follow it with a morsel of food so small that thirty or forty pieces will not fill up your dog. Snap the clicker only when the dog's attention is on something besides food; never snap it or feed him when he begs. Soon, whenever the dog hears the click, he will drop whatever he is doing and run to you for food.

Now you are ready to shape his behavior. Reinforce your dog with the clicker and a morsel of food each time his behavior is reasonably close to what you want. If you want him to turn round and round, click and feed him when he makes a slight movement to the right. Gradually, demand that he turn farther and farther to the right before you reinforce him. Never touch your dog or speak to him while you are training him. The sound and the food must be your only contacts with him. With patience, you will have your dog dancing in a circle.

Dogs have been trained for centuries, but until recently few people have trained pigeons. Today, in laboratories all over the country, pigeons in small boxes learn by this same method. The box is not much bigger than the pigeon, and inside it are a lever and a tray. When the pigeon pecks the lever at the right moment, a food pellet drops into the tray.

B. F. Skinner, the Harvard psychologist who invented this box that other psychologists use to train small animals, has taught pigeons to bowl, to play "Take Me Out to the Ball Game" on the xylophone, and to play a rousing game of Ping-Pong. Skinner shapes his pigeons' behavior just as you might shape the behavior of your dog, and his methods are just as simple.

He taught his two pigeon Ping-Pong experts separately.

First he fastened a Ping-Pong ball to the edge of the table and fed the hungry bird each time it pecked the ball. Next he unfastened the ball so that it would roll away when the pigeon pecked it. If the pigeon pecked the ball hard enough, it struck a bar that released more food. After each pigeon learned to peck the ball sharply each time it came near, Skinner brought the two Ping-Pong players together.

He used a table about sixteen inches long with metal rails that kept the ball from rolling off the sides. To begin the game, Skinner would place a ball in the center of the table. When it rolled toward one pigeon, the bird would peck it and the rally was under way. Sometimes there would be as many as five or six returns of the ball before one of the pigeons scored a point. Whenever a pigeon pecked the ball hard enough to send it flying off the opposite end of the table, the ball tripped a switch that fed the triumphant player. If that scoring system doesn't sound familiar, recall that when you play the game, you are rewarded with a point each time you send the ball past your opponent.

People don't press bars for their dinner, but they do learn to repeat behavior that they find pleasant or that gets them something they want. Imagine a mother who picks up her baby whenever it cries but does not pick it up at other times. Perhaps she says to herself, "Don't bother the baby when he is good." Babies, being reasonably bright animals, soon learn that one cries to get a little contact comfort. The mother is reinforcing her baby for crying. She is making a crybaby of him.

Now suppose that she discovers what she has done and decides to break the baby's habit. She no longer picks him up when he cries. If she allows him to cry long enough, she thinks, he will no longer be rewarded for crying and will stop. She wants his constant crying to undergo *extinction*, which is what psychologists say takes place when an animal or person no longer gets the expected reward for his behavior. He stops doing it.

But this mother must be careful or she will find herself in trouble. If she allows her well-fed, dry, and comfortable baby to cry and cry, he will stop after a while. It may take forty-five minutes, but he will stop. The next time he cries, she again manages to outwait him. But the third time she has visitors and, after a few minutes of his wailing and her guests' concerned looks, she hurries to the crib and picks him up. She has just put her baby on a schedule of *intermittent reinforcement* and destroyed all her hard work.

In intermittent reinforcement, sometimes animals get their rewards and sometimes they don't, but they never know when the reward is due. Psychologists have learned that animals that are rewarded intermittently keep up their learned behavior for a long time after all rewards have been taken away. Skinner tells about the pigeon in his laboratory that pecked a key for food 10,000 times before it gave up. The explanation is simple: these animals have learned to respond even when no reinforcement comes. In human terms, we might say they have learned to hope and they will keep on hoping until they learn to despair.

Intermittent reinforcement works on adults just as it works on pigeons, rats, and babies. Two notorious examples of intermittent reinforcement are fishing and gambling. No fisherman expects to get a fish each time he casts his line, and the economy of Las Vegas is based upon the knowledge that a gambler who has won occasionally will keep on betting even when he loses heavily. We might describe a slot machine as a Skinner box for human beings.

If that mother wants to stop her baby's unreasonable crying

even faster, she will reinforce his good behavior by picking him up when he is awake but quiet. Spoiled babies are not the babies who have been picked up and held too often; they are the babies who have been picked up only when they cried. Children give their parents the kind of behavior that the parents reward.

Learning in laboratories — and in life — is not always fun. Psychologists sometimes use *negative reinforcement* to make an animal learn. When Neal Miller taught his rats to open a door to escape from an electric shock, he was using negative reinforcement. The rats learned to get away from the shock by doing what Miller wanted them to do.

Negative reinforcement is different from *punishment,* which we all know about. Punishment comes after you do something and is supposed to teach you not to repeat whatever terrible thing you did. Studies with animals show that punishment just after an animal presses a bar does indeed make the animal stop bar-pressing. But if food comes along with the punishment, the animal will stop its bar-pressing only as long as the punishment is kept up. When experimenters stop punishing rats with electric shock, the rats go back to pressing the bar as fast as they did before. This effect is familiar to anyone who knows children who behave perfectly around their parents but break every rule when they are away from home.

Often punishment comes too late. When the dog that steals the steak from the kitchen gets whipped, his punishment comes after the steak has reinforced his theft. And the dog that gets spanked when he comes home after chasing cars has been punished for coming home.

It is possible to change behavior with any of these methods. If your father tells you that he will give you a bicycle if you stop biting your nails, he is offering positive reinforcement. If he tells you that you must stay home every night until you stop biting your nails, he is using negative reinforcement. (You escape from home by learning not to bite your nails.) If he tells you he will beat you if you keep biting your nails, he is threatening you with punishment.

Whenever an animal is reinforced, it tends to repeat whatever it was doing when it got its reward. If an animal has been pressing a bar for food, that makes sense. But sometimes the behavior has nothing to do with the reward. For example, if a pigeon has its head tucked under its wing when food drops into the cup, it is likely to tuck its head back under its wing to get more food.

People do the same thing. We call it superstitious behavior. Watch a baseball game. Before he steps to the plate, nearly every batter makes a special gesture: he tugs at his cap, he spits, he shuffles his foot across the left side of the plate, he rubs his nose. At some time in the past, the batter made his particular gesture just before he smacked a ball over the fence. Because our response to intermittent reinforcement is so strong, the baseball player, the gambler, and the fisherman all tend to develop odd rituals that they have connected with success.

It may be that the development of tribal rituals comes about in the same way. Once a tribe happened to be dancing and the rain began to fall. They began to dance more often, which increased the chances that they would be dancing when it rained. A ritual was born, and the rain continued to fall — on a schedule of intermittent reinforcement — after other rain dances.

But learning is more than making simple responses to simple stimuli. Wolfgang Köhler showed that rats can learn relationships; they can learn to choose the correct object by learning the relationship between two — or more — objects. He discovered this ability almost by accident.

Köhler placed rats before two doors, one painted light gray and one painted dark gray. If the rat jumped to the light gray door, it opened and the rat found food. If the rat jumped to the dark gray door, the door stayed closed, and the rat bumped its nose and fell into a net below. The rats quickly learned to jump only to the light gray door.

Then Köhler changed the dark gray door to white. The rats stopped jumping toward the light gray door — where the food had always been — and jumped to the white door. Puzzled, Köhler switched doors again. This time he used a black door and a dark gray door. The rats jumped toward the same dark gray door that had sent them falling into the nets before and that they had learned to avoid. But at last the rats' intentions were clear. Instead of learning to jump to a light gray door and to shun a dark gray door, they had learned to jump to the lighter of two stimuli.

In Harry and Margaret Harlow's laboratories, monkeys have learned the concepts of *alike* and *different*. Psychologists performed a series of experiments in which little monkeys had to make the right choice to earn raisins. The researchers put three objects in front of a monkey's cage. Two of the objects were alike and one was different. Under the different object waited a raisin. At first the monkey lifted the objects randomly — sometimes it had to lift all three objects to find the raisin. But gradually it learned to look for the different object. If two wooden triangles and a wooden circle lay before it, the monkey went straight to the circle. But if two circles and one triangle were in front of the cage, the monkey immediately lifted the triangle.

Animals and human beings store concepts and relationships

in their brains. They transfer to one situation what they learn in another. If they did not, no one would ever learn general categories, such as toys, automobiles, animals, or machines. Nor would they be able to apply such concepts as up, down, alike, different, heavy, light, red, or blue.

All those pigeons pecking all those Ping-Pong balls have led to radical changes in the way human beings are taught. The principles of teaching machines are the same principles that Skinner uses with pigeons and Sea World uses with dolphins. The machine's program shapes a student's behavior as surely as the Skinner box shapes the antics of a pigeon.

First, the program arranges the environment so the student will make a correct first response. He reads a question so simple that he will answer it correctly. The student gets immediate reinforcement by learning that his answer is right. Then, by small steps, he gradually answers harder and harder questions. Each question gives him new information and reinforces him for the right answer. Because the program does not rely on group lectures, each student can move at his own pace. The slow student can take his time, and the fast one can work without being bored. A question must be answered correctly before the machine will move to the next question. Teaching machine records report class and individual progress to the instructor. At the same time, the records tell him which questions are too difficult and need to be changed.

In Palo Alto, California, children learn to read and to do arithmetic by computer. In the reading program, designed by psychologist Richard Atkinson, each first grader sits in front of his own computer terminal. In front of him is a small screen, a cathode-ray tube — much like a television picture tube — and a typewriter keyboard. He puts on a pair of earphones and picks up a light-pen — a light-sensitive pen that "talks" to the computer when the first grader touches it to the face of the cathode-ray tube.

Through the earphones, the student hears a word, perhaps *fan*. At the same time, a picture of a fan flashes on the screen and the word *fan* appears on the cathode-ray tube. Next a series of words appears on the tube, and the student must touch his light-pen to the correct square on the tube to show the computer that he can read the word *fan*. If the student touches the wrong square, the computer will tell him — by means of a recorded voice in the earphones — that his answer is wrong and help him to find the right answer. If his answer is right, the computer will tell him so and move on to the next question.

As children learn to read and write, they begin to talk to the computer by typing on the keyboard.

You don't need a computer to use programmed instruction. Educators have put programmed courses into textbooks that students use much as you would use a workbook. The student answers a question, uncovers the correct answer and — if he is right — goes on to the next question. If he is wrong, the book directs him to another section of questions designed for persons who need extra help.

Students can learn more than the facts of history or the multiplication tables from computers. With the skillful use of questions, principles and concepts can also be taught. But installing computers in every classroom will not send teachers to the unemployment office. Instead, it will free them for more creative teaching and will allow them to give individual attention to the children in their classes.

Memory

6

WITH MUCH GROANING and head-scratching, you memorize a list of twenty-five spelling words or the parts of the digestive system or the powers of Congress. With less effort you learn a new dance step, the horsepower of a Corvette, or the batting averages of your favorite baseball team. How do you store all this information inside your body until the test next month or the baseball season next year or for the rest of your life?

Psychologists have not been able to agree on just what happens inside your body when you learn, but they have come up with several interesting theories. Some years ago, neurosurgeon Wilder Penfield conducted a series of experiments in Montreal. Brain surgery often takes place under local anaesthesia: the patient is awake but feels no pain. When Penfield operated on the brain under these conditions, he would stimulate sections of the brain with weak currents of electricity. When his electric probe touched the temporal lobe, many of his patients would relive things that had happened to them. A patient might, as he had as a child, run through a field knee-deep with daisies. At the same time that he relived — and not just remembered — his run through the daisies, he knew that he was lying on an operating table in Montreal with his brain exposed.

On hand during those operations was a young psychologist,

D. O. Hebb, who later developed one of the major theories of brain function. Hebb — and many other psychologists — believes that when we learn, physical changes take place in our nervous systems.

Each neuron, the basic cell in the nervous system, looks rather like a limp tree without leaves. The central part of the cell ends in many branchlike tendrils called *dendrites,* while the long trunk, or *axon,* divides into rootlike *end-branches.* The dendrites of one neuron lie close to the end-branches of other neurons, and electrical or chemical signals pass across this gap, called a *synapse,* from one neuron to another.

Some psychologists believe that as we memorize spelling words, for example, a change takes place in the way one neuron excites another. As we study the words and go over them again and again, we set up what Hebb calls a *cell assembly* — a group of cells that fire quickly in turn, like a string of snapping mousetraps, to trigger the memory. As the neurons fire again and again in the same pattern, some change takes place that makes it easier for the same circuit of neurons to respond. Hebb compares the memory process to a switchboard, with the brain acting as a telephone exchange to connect incoming and outgoing cell assemblies.

Hebb's theory of cell assemblies can account for a kind of learning that operant conditioning cannot explain. Both human beings and animals learn without making any kind of response and without getting any kind of reward. This kind of learning is called *latent learning.*

B. Hymovitch raised rats in wire-mesh cages so tiny that the rats could not move about. Some lived in cages placed so that they could see the laboratory and watch what went on there. Others lived in the same kind of lighted cages, but could see nothing of their surroundings. When the rats were grown, the rats that had always seen the laboratory learned to run mazes much faster and made fewer mistakes than the rats that had not been able to see the room about them. In the same way, the baby that lies in its crib and watches the family move about the room is learning without response or reward.

Latent learning is a part of your daily life. Suppose you walk through a room and notice a pencil lying on a table. You make no response, but if a friend asks you later for a pencil, you immediately go and get it for him. In a similar manner, if you pass a clock, you notice the time of day and can repeat the information if someone should ask for it. In Hebb's theory, during latent learning changes take place in the brain's transmission paths, making one set of cell assemblies more complicated or connecting several sets together.

Other psychologists explain memory differently. Instead of seeing it as a switchboard process, Karl Pribram sees it as a hologram. A hologram is a unique kind of photograph: each object appears solid and three-dimensional, and by moving your head, you can see around and behind it. A holographic film does not store a scene in the usual way, with each point on the film recording a particular part of the scene. Instead, many points on the holographic film store the entire scene. If you cut a holographic film apart, you can reproduce the entire picture from any fragment of the film. This theory suggests that the body stores information in several places. It helps explain why persons with extensive brain damage often keep their memories and function as if their brains were undamaged. (To allow for this retention of memory, Hebb's theory requires the brain to set up several cell assemblies for each memory.)

One of the most interesting — and controversial — memory experiments took place in Ann Arbor, Michigan, where James

McConnell works with worms. His worms are planarians, small flatworms less than an inch long, which live in rivers and ponds all over the world. These worms respond to operant conditioning just as dogs or rats or people do, and McConnell taught his planarians always to turn right when put into a T-shaped maze. After his worms had learned their lessons, he cut them in two. Planarians regenerate. That is, if you cut one worm into two pieces, each piece grows back into a complete, healthy worm. When the planarians were again hale and hearty, McConnell put them back into the T-maze. He discovered that both worms, whether they were originally tail or head, learned much faster than new, untaught worms to turn right when they came to the cross-corridor of the maze. This meant that the information was stored not in the worm's head, but throughout its body.

McConnell thought about this for a while and devised a new experiment. He ground up some worms that had learned to turn right in the maze and fed them to other worms. The cannibal worms that ate their educated brothers learned to turn right in the maze much faster than other cannibal worms that had eaten uneducated worms. The first experiment surprised everyone; the second startled them. Because the worms had been pulverized, psychologists deduced that learning might take place at a chemical level, that when a worm learned something, a chemical inside its body cells changed permanently in some way.

McConnell thinks that RNA, the same chemical that — as a messenger of DNA — determines whether a forming baby will have red or black hair, brown or blue eyes, is the memory chemical. RNA, which is manufactured by DNA, occurs in most living cells. Some researchers suspect that when an animal or a person learns something, RNA somehow stores it.

There is support for this theory. When experimenters take RNA from trained worms and inject it into untrained worms, the untrained worms appear to remember what the trained worms had learned — or at least they learn their lesson much faster than other worms. And if planarians get their lessons while they are in water containing a chemical that destroys RNA, they can neither learn nor remember.

McConnell's work with planarians is controversial because it has been difficult to repeat his experiments and come up with the same results. While some psychologists have done this, others have not been able to do so. In addition, some psychologists believe that McConnell's cannibal worms did not get any memories with their dinner, but instead got the general ability to learn. They say that his planarians did not remember to turn right in the maze; they just learned their navigation lesson faster than the worms in the control group.

But research with rats shows that when a rat learns a specific task, say to climb a wire in order to get its dinner, the RNA molecules in its brain change. Perhaps one day a new theory of learning will resolve the controversy and explain both the firing of neurons and the role of chemicals in our storage of memories.

While we don't know precisely what happens inside our bodies when we store memories, we can discover a lot about the conditions that make learning easier or harder by watching people's behavior. All learning involves memory, but not all memory is alike. When you look up a telephone number, you remember the seven digits while you are dialing. But if you want to call the same person back, you find that you must look up the number again — even if you made the first call only a few minutes before. You stored that number in what psychologists call your *short-term memory*.

Now suppose you want to call your best friend. You pick up the phone and dial his number immediately. His number is stored in your *long-term memory,* where you keep the names of family and friends, the multiplication tables, and everything you remember, from the color of the sweater you wore yesterday to the shape of the teddy bear you played with when you were two.

There is another kind of memory that appears in children and in a very few adults. This is *eidetic memory,* a true photographic memory. The eidetiker does not just remember exactly what he has seen, but sees it again, with all of its original color and detail, as if a movie projector had flashed it onto a screen. When Ralph Haber tested 500 schoolchildren, he found 20 with some eidetic memory. After they looked at a picture from *Alice in Wonderland,* for example, they would describe details from the picture as if it were before their eyes. When asked how many stripes the Cheshire cat had on its tail, the eidetic child would count the stripes.

Eidetic ability usually fades as a child grows up, but now and again an adult keeps his photographic memory. At Harvard, Charles Stromeyer tested a young Harvard teacher whose eidetic memories did not fade rapidly, as do the memories of most eidetikers.

Stromeyer used stereograms in his experiments. A stereogram works much like the solid, three-dimensional picture that appears when one looks through a viewer that presents a slightly different picture to each eye. The three-dimensional stereogram — usually of a simple shape such as a T floating above a square or a triangle that appears to be at the bottom of a pit — appears when each eye sees a different pattern of dots. Until the two patterns are viewed together, both pictures are meaningless jumbles of dots.

On the first day of these tests, the Harvard teacher looked at one of the stereogram pictures with only her right eye. She looked at it for three minutes, then rested, then looked at it again for three minutes, then rested, until she had looked at the picture for twelve minutes. On the second day, she looked at the other picture with her left eye and then projected the previous day's eidetic image on top of it. Within ten seconds she saw the stereogram — a floating square. As you might guess, she had found her eidetic talent extremely helpful in studying for examinations, in memorizing poetry, and in learning foreign languages.

Although most of us don't have photographic memories, our long-term memories work well enough. They work so well that we become aware of them only when we forget a fact or a face we think we should have remembered.

A major reason for forgetting is simply the failure to learn. When you meet a stranger and later can't remember his name, it's because you did not learn his name when you were introduced. If you had looked carefully at the person and repeated his name several times in the conversation, you would have remembered it. But you treated the name just as you treat a telephone number you don't expect to use again, and it never moved from short- to long-term memory.

Much of the same thing happens when you cannot answer the questions on a test. If you have only read the textbook several times, you have probably learned little. And if you have just stared at your notes and gazed out the window, you have probably learned nothing. In order to learn, you must study, and study is an active process. It means that you must memorize, that you ask yourself questions and answer them, that you practice recalling important information, and that you understand the principles that underlie the material.

A. I. Gates gave a group of students a list of nonsense syllables to learn. The list consisted of syllables like *VEL, GOP,
ZUK, YUV.* He divided the students into five groups. The
first group read the syllables to themselves over and over
again. The second group read the syllables 80 percent of the
time and practiced reciting them 20 percent of the time; the
third group read 60 percent of the time and recited 40 percent
of the time; the fourth group read 40 percent and recited 60
percent; the last group read only 20 percent of the time and
spent 80 percent of the time reciting the syllables.

Four hours after the study period was over, Gates tested all
the students. He found that the more time they had spent reciting, the more syllables they remembered. The students who
had recited 80 percent of the time remembered more than
three times as many syllables as the students who had spent all
their time reading.

Most of us think that we forget material just because we
don't use it, but few experiments support this theory. If the
theory of disuse were true, you would forget how to swim or
ski or ice-skate from one season to the next. But something
must account for the fact that we do forget things we have
learned. Most psychologists belive that, while there is some
decay of memory with the passage of time, what happens to us
between the time we learn and the time we try to remember
plays an important role in forgetting.

K. Dallenbach and J. G. Jenkins ran a memory experiment
at Cornell University. Two students acted as guinea pigs. For
two months the students reported to the lab, where they
learned lists of nonsense syllables. Afterward, they sometimes
went about their daily activities: going to class, reading, walking, playing tennis, whatever they normally would do. At

other times they would learn the syllables and then go to sleep.

Every time, Jenkins and Dallenbach would test the students one, two, four, and eight hours after they learned the syllables. The results were always the same: when they had slept, the students remembered more than when they had done other things. For example, eight hours after they learned a list of ten nonsense syllables, they would remember five or six of them if they had slept. But if they had gone about the campus on their normal business, they would remember only one of the syllables. Jenkins and Dallenbach decided that *intervening activity* — what we do between the time we learn and the time we try to remember — interferes with memory and causes forgetting.

Twenty years after Dallenbach tested the Cornell students, he and H. Minami taught cockroaches to stay away from one corner of their cage by giving them electric shocks each time they reached that corner. Then the researchers placed half the cockroaches in a dark, damp place, where they stayed motionless. The rest of the cockroaches were put on a treadmill in a dry, well-lighted cage; these cockroaches moved about most of the time. If disuse alone caused a loss of memory, both groups of cockroaches would have forgotten about the shock that waited for them in the corner of the cage.

When the researchers put the cockroaches back in their usual cage, a few of those that had stayed in the quiet, dark place forgot and strayed into the wired section, but many more of the active cockroaches wandered over to be shocked. As time passed, more and more of the cockroaches that had never been shut up ventured into the corner and got electric shocks, but most of the cockroaches from the dark stayed well

away from that corner of the cage. The behavior of the cockroaches showed the same principle of interference that psychologists see at work in human beings.

Other experiments have shown that what we do *before* we
learn also interferes with memory. B. J. Underwood compared
different memory studies and found that the differences in forgetting varied wildly from one study to the next. When he examined the research carefully, he found that the more memorizing of the same kind the subjects had done before the
experiments, the more they forgot. If they had learned lists of
nonsense syllables before, they would do poorly on lists of
nonsense syllables; if they had learned pairs of numbers before, they would do poorly with lists of number pairs.

Some psychologists believe that this kind of interference
helps to explain memory differences between the young and
the old. Young children have had few experiences, so they remember in great detail things that happen to them. Old people have had years of experience and learning that interferes
with their memories of recent events.

Taking a nap after we study or studying just before bedtime
will help cut memory loss, but it's not practical to go to sleep
after every event we want to remember. Psychologists have
found other methods, however, that will cut down on the
memory loss that takes place because we are awake and active
most of the time.

The important thing, of course, is to move information we
wish to keep from our short- to our long-term memories. It
appears that *rehearsal* — going over the material in some way,
such as reciting or thinking about it — helps us to store information in our long-term memories. It also appears that our
brains need time to fix that information permanently in our
memories. Accident cases show how this works. If a person

has a head injury, often he cannot remember what happened just before the accident. This *retrograde amnesia* apparently comes about when a blow disrupts the process that transfers information into the long-term memory.

J. L. McGaugh has used electric shock to create retrograde amnesia in rats. He placed a rat on a small platform just above the floor. When put on this perch, rats normally step off to the floor. McGaugh ran an electric current through the floor, and when the rat put its paw down, it got a shock. The next day, the rat stayed on the platform, having learned that the floor was painful.

Now McGaugh placed a new rat on the platform. The rat put its paw on the electrified floor and hastily drew back. As soon as it was back on the platform, McGaugh sent an electric shock through its head from one side to the other. The shock was so strong that it threw the rat into convulsions. The next day, the rat stepped from the platform as if it had never learned that the floor was painful.

Rehearsal is vital when we need to retain information, but just how much? Research shows that *overlearning* — continuing to study after you have mastered the material — increases the amount that you later remember. If you are memorizing a list of German words or Newton's laws of motion, you generally stop studying once you can repeat them without a mistake. But if you will go on and recite them a few more times, your memory will be much better than if you stop after the first perfect recitation.

It is also much easier to learn material that you understand. As you might guess, studies show that three-letter words are easier to remember than three-letter nonsense syllables, and that meaningful sentences are easier to remember than random strings of words such as "byway consequence handsomely plutocrat bent flux orchestra swiftness weather-beaten existed."

Sometimes we must memorize lists of words or of numbers that have little meaning. For centuries, people have relied on *mnemonics* — artificial aids to memory. You probably learned in music that *Every Good Boy Does Fine* tells you the lines of the staff, while *FACE* tells the spaces. Medical students repeat, "On Old Olympus' Towering Top, A Fat Ancient German Vaults And Hops," to remind them of the twelve pairs of cranial nerves: Olfactory, Optic, Oculomotor, Trochlear, Trigeminal, Abducent, Facial, Auditory, Glossopharyngeal, Vagus, Accessory, Hypoglossal. Each word in the sentence begins with the same letter as one of the nerves. And if you are interested in physics, the name "Roy G. Biv" will tell you the correct order of colors in the spectrum: red, orange, yellow, green, blue, indigo, and violet.

The Russian psychologist Aleksander Luria studied a man with a phenomenal memory. Thirty years after he memorized lists of words, he could repeat them without making a single error. In order to remember, the man would think of a visual image that represented the word and then mentally place it somewhere along a street. When he recalled the words, he would imagine walking along the street and would name the things he saw in his walk. The same technique was used by Mark Twain and by ancient Greeks, who would imagine a familiar house and place objects they wanted to remember in the different rooms.

There is obviously more to memory than meaning — whether real or artificial. Motivation, it turns out, plays a strong role in our memories. We tend to remember pleasant events and to forget unpleasant ones. Sigmund Freud, the father of psychoanalysis, noticed that his patients seemed to forget events that made them anxious. *Seemed* to forget. Freud believed that his patients did not forget these events; they just pushed the memories into their unconscious — a process he called *repression*. He suggested that repressed memories lie beneath most mental illness.

Psychologist H. Meltzer tested Freud's theory. He thought that if Freud was correct, people would remember pleasant experiences longer than they remembered unpleasant ones. Just after Christmas vacation, Meltzer asked a group of college students to write down what had happened to them over the holidays and to say whether each memory was pleasant or unpleasant. Six weeks later, Meltzer again asked the same group of students to list their holiday memories. The second time they recorded their memories, their lists were shorter than before, and the students remembered more pleasant events than unpleasant ones.

Meltzer's experiment supports Freud's theory but does not prove that it is true or that it is the only factor in forgetting. We may forget if we don't want to remember. However, this study does not show whether the students repressed their unpleasant memories or whether they truly forgot them.

Sometimes changes within our bodies affect memory. Donald Overton used negative reinforcement to train rats in a T-maze. He shocked their paws until they ran down the right-hand corridor. After they had learned to make the right-hand turn, he gave them so much pentobarbital — a common drug that physicians prescribe for patients who cannot sleep — that they could hardly drag themselves through the maze. The pentobarbital affected their memories, and they forgot all about taking the right-hand turn. While they were drugged, Overton used electric shock to make them take the left-hand corridor. Despite their groggy state, the rats quickly learned to turn left each time they were put into the maze.

Later Overton put the rats back into the maze. Sometimes they were full of pentobarbital, other times they were in a normal, alert state. Each time the rats were drugged, they turned left; each time they were undrugged, they turned right. Apparently their memories were somehow connected with their physiological state: when drugged, they remembered what they had learned under drugs and forgot what they had learned while in a normal state; when undrugged, they remembered what they had learned without drugs and forgot what they had learned while drugged.

This kind of learning is called *state-dependent learning*. The animal's ability to perform whatever act it learns is linked to its physical condition at the time it learns the response.

Alcohol and tranquilizers have the same effects on animals as pentobarbital and other barbiturates. And high doses of these drugs appear to have similar effects on man. The person who wakes up after drinking heavily and cannot remember what he did the night before is a familiar example. Donald Goodwin reproduced this effect in the laboratory. He gave college students eight to ten ounces of vodka in mixed drinks. The students showed the same state-dependent learning as the rats in tests of word memory, but, when sober, recognized pictures they had seen while drunk. Perhaps alcohol does not affect all kinds of memory in the same way. Our memory for what we have seen may not be as sensitive to the effects of alcohol as our memory for what we have heard or read. Another study indicates that students who take amphetamines to keep awake while cramming for exams may forget what they have learned once the drug wears off.

While we still have much to learn about memory, we know enough to realize that it is not always trustworthy. When witnesses in the courtroom tell very different versions of the same event, it is quite probable that no one is lying. Each swears to his own version of the truth. Without realizing it, he often makes what he saw fit what he believes. When a psychology instructor arranges for someone to interrupt his class with a staged, violent scene, he finds that his students cannot agree on either the appearance of the actors or just what each one did during the performance.

This is why eyewitness testimony is notoriously unreliable. All the factors that affect our memories when we try to memorize nonsense syllables are at work when we try to recall an event we have witnessed. Interference, time, and our emotions combine to prevent us from remembering accurately, and the more our emotions are involved, the less accurate our memories are likely to be.

Thinking

7

WHEN WORLD WAR I broke out, a German psychologist was stranded on an island off the coast of Africa. Wolfgang Köhler spent his four-year exile studying the chimpanzees that lived on the island, and his studies tell us a lot about chimpanzees — and about man.

In one experiment, Nueva, a female chimpanzee was alone in a cage. Outside the cage — just beyond Nueva's reach — Köhler placed some bananas. Nueva stretched her arm through the bars and tried to grasp the fruit, but it was too far away. When Nueva realized she could not reach the bananas, she stuck out her lower lip, looked at Köhler as if to beg him for the fruit, and whimpered. Then she threw herself on the ground and lay on her back, the picture of despair. After about seven minutes, Nueva got up, snatched a stick that lay just outside the bars, and pulled the bananas within reach.

It seemed to Köhler that Nueva suddenly saw the problem of getting a banana in an entirely different way. Earlier she had used the stick to scratch in the dirt and to push banana skins into a heap. Now when she looked at the stick and at the bananas, she realized that — used in a different way — the stick would bring her the tantalizing fruit.

Köhler called this kind of behavior *insight,* and it is a complex kind of learning. The apes on that African island showed insight on other occasions. One day Köhler suspended a bunch of bananas from the top of the cage. No matter how the chimpanzee Grande stretched or jumped, he could not reach the hanging fruit. In Aesop's fable, the fox that could not reach the hanging grapes decided that the fruit was probably sour and not worth eating. But Köhler's chimpanzee was made of sterner stuff.

On the floor of the cage lay several wooden boxes. When his jumping failed, Grande began to walk about the cage. Back and forth, back and forth he paced. Suddenly he stopped in front of the boxes, piled them under the fruit, and climbed them like a ladder to reach the bananas. With a flash of insight, the chimpanzee had seen the boxes as a ladder or staircase.

Some people call the moment of insight an "Aha!" experience. When it comes, the chimpanzee — or the person — suddenly sees the elements of a problem in a new relationship. You use insight when you solve an algebra problem or when you discover what caused a puzzling motor failure in the family car. Often, once you have had your moment of insight, the solution to the problem seems obvious, and you wonder why you didn't think of it before.

Insight does not strike from the heavens, even though its sudden arrival might lead us to assume that it does. Insight depends upon past experience, which means that it comes from previous learning. If you did not know something about an internal-combustion engine, you could not discover why the car won't run. If you had no previous algebra instruction, you could not solve the tricky problem.

Even the chimpanzees' insights about banana gathering depended upon their past experience. Herbert G. Birch tested six chimpanzees that had been born in captivity. One at a time, he put them into a cage, put a stick within reach, and placed bananas outside the bars. Only one chimpanzee, Jojo, had played with sticks before. Jojo had his moment of insight and used his stick to pull the bananas to him. One other chimpanzee, Bard, also got his bananas after he accidentally brushed against the stick. When the stick moved the fruit, Bard grasped the stick and raked the bananas within reach. But no matter how long they tried, the other four chimpanzees failed to discover that the stick could be used as a food-gathering tool.

Birch then allowed all the chimpanzees to play with sticks for three days. They used the sticks to poke the researcher and each other, but not once in the three days did they use the sticks as rakes. Again Birch put his six chimpanzees in the cage, one at a time. The stick lay within reach, the bananas at a distance. Within twenty seconds, each chimpanzee used his stick to rake the bananas to him. Until the chimpanzees had had experience playing with sticks, they could solve the banana problem only by accident.

Our ability to solve problems rests on past experience, but other factors also affect our thinking and help or hinder our problem-solving. Before a person can solve a problem, he must recognize all the elements that make it up. Until Nueva saw that the stick could be a rake as well as a tool to scratch in the dirt, she could not use it to get bananas.

Psychologist N. R. F. Maier tested the ability of human beings to see new uses for familiar objects. Maier took a student into a room and asked him to tie together two cords that hung from the ceiling. The student grasped one cord and grabbed for the other, but it was just out of reach. He looked around the room and saw a chair, a pair of pliers, and a few other objects. First he brought the chair over, stood on it, and tried to grab the second string. It was still too far away.

When the student failed to solve the problem, Maier walked over to the window and brushed against the cord that hung from the venetian blinds. The cord swung back and forth. Suddenly the student picked up the pliers, tied them to the end of one cord, set it swinging, grasped the other cord, and — when the swinging cord came within reach — grabbed it and tied the two ends together. The sight of the swaying cord at the window had caused the student to see the elements of the problem in a new light.

Sometimes our past experience stands in the way of solving problems. We use an object like a pair of pliers in one way and find it difficult to see them in another role — in this case as a pendulum weight. Herbert Birch, who gave sticks to six chimpanzees, also asked students to tie strings together. But he approached the experiment in a different way. He divided the students into two groups. Before he showed the strings to a person in the first group, he asked him to finish wiring an electrical circuit by installing a *switch*. Before anyone from the second group saw the dangling strings, he had to finish wiring an electrical circuit by installing a *relay*.

The problem was the same. The strings were too far apart to reach unless the student weighted one of the strings and set it swinging. In the room were an electrical switch and a relay — either of them would serve nicely as a pendulum weight. The students who had wired switches into the circuit tended to solve the problem by tying the relay to the string; the students who had wired relays into the circuit tended to tie the switch onto the string. Using an object in one way made it unlikely that the students would see that object in another role. Psychologists call this *functional fixedness*, because a person becomes so fixed on one function of a tool or an object that he finds other uses "unthinkable."

Set is a similar habit that interferes with problem-solving. When we find a successful way of doing something, we become rigid in our approach. Instead of fixing upon an object's use, we fix upon a method of responding to a problem. Set often causes us to make a hard problem out of an easy one.

A. S. Luchins used arithmetic problems to test thousands of persons for set. In one group of problems, he told them to suppose that they had three empty jars of different sizes. The problem was to get a certain amount of water by filling and emptying the jars. For example, suppose you have a jar that holds 127 quarts, another that holds 21 quarts, and a third that holds three quarts. You need 100 quarts. The easiest way to solve the problem is to fill the 127-quart jar, then pour out enough water to fill the 21-quart jar once and the 3-quart jar twice. Presto! 100 quarts.

Most persons can solve this problem without much difficulty. But Luchins found that if he gave his puzzle-solvers a series of problems that could be solved in the same way (fill the largest jar once, pour the second jar full once and the third jar full twice), something odd happened to their problem-solving ability. He asked them to produce 25 quarts of water using a 76-quart jar, a 28-quart jar, and a 3-quart jar. Two thirds of the people who solved all the difficult problems could not figure out a way to get 25 quarts of water. They had become so set on filling the large jar first and working from it, that they could not see that all they had to do was to fill the 28-quart jar and pour out enough water to fill the 3-quart jar once.

Logical thinking is an important tool in problem-solving. A person uses logic to put together all the information that bears on a problem. Often, however, set corrupts logical thinking and traps a person into reaching a wrong conclusion. If we know that all the members of the chemistry class are intelligent, and we also know that all good students are intelligent, we are tempted to say, "All members of the chemistry class are good students." But intelligence is no guarantee that a person will attend class, read the textbook, or study the assignment.

When our emotions are involved, we sometimes accept such errors of logic. Our political beliefs often distort our judgment so that we eagerly accept wrong conclusions. Suppose someone tells you, "All members of the John Birch Society are conservative. Barry Goldwater is conservative. I'm sure that Barry Goldwater is a member of the John Birch Society." If you are a liberal, you may find the argument appealing. But if you're a conservative, you'll be more likely to believe a friend who says, "All Communists want the United States out of Vietnam. Jane Fonda wants the United States out of Vietnam. I'm sure that Jane Fonda is a Communist." The argument is the same in both cases, but it is identical with the argument, "All cows are animals. Your dog is an animal. That means your dog is a cow." Politicians often try to persuade voters that dogs are cows.

Sometimes we face a problem that logical thinking cannot solve. The problem demands an original response, one that is not obvious if we look carefully at all parts of the problem. This kind of problem demands *associational thinking,* a relaxed flow of ideas that lets us think about the familiar in a new, perhaps strange way. Daydreaming is associational thinking, and so is the thought of our night dreams; our minds drift from one image to another without the distraction of logical thought.

Many psychologists believe that associational thinking is closely linked with creativity. They believe that scientists, mathematicians, painters, poets, playwrights, and novelists use associational thinking to come up with new ideas. Most first-hand reports from original thinkers indicate that the ideas for their discoveries just pop into their heads, which indicates that the psychologists are probably right.

Karl Friedrich Gauss, who pushed forward mathematical theory, said that his solution came like a sudden flash of lightning. Friedrich Kekule, who worked out the molecular structure of benzene, dreamed of a snake biting its tail and suddenly realized that the benzene molecule must be a closed ring. Writers often think about their problems of plot or character just before they go to sleep at night and wake up in the morning with the problems solved.

Psychologists have tried to develop tests for creative thinking and have found that creativity is extremely difficult to study in the laboratory. Most tests for creativity seem to be tests to reveal the absence of set. For example, a psychologist will ask you how many uses you can think of for a familiar object like a pair of pliers or a brick. Or he might ask you to use several common objects to solve a problem that requires you to use one or more of the objects in a new way.

Another test depends upon your ability to make remote associations. You are given three words that seem to have nothing in common and must come up with a fourth that is related to all the other three. For example, what word goes with *collar, fly,* and *hobby?* The word you are looking for is *horse* (horsecollar, horsefly, hobbyhorse). If you'd like to test yourself for flexibility and originality, try this sample from the Mednich Remote Association Test.

1. stool powder ball   [foot]
2. blue cake cottage   [cheese]
3. motion poke down   [slow]
4. line birthday surprise   [party]
5. house village golf   [green]
6. card knee rope   [trick]
7. news doll tiger   [paper]
8. bull tired hot   [dog]
9. spelling line busy   [bee]
10. painting bowl nail   [finger]

Suppose you score high on the remote association test, are not especially bound by set or functional fixedness, and can think logically. Can we say that, if you have the necessary experience, you can solve a very difficult problem? It all depends upon another factor that enters into most human endeavors — motivation. Some goal must arouse your interest, or your problem-solving ability will drop to almost nothing. Your mind will wander and the slightest noise will distract you.

The stronger your motivation, the faster you will solve your problem — up to a certain point. If the goal is extremely important to you and your motivation becomes too intense, your thought concentrates on the goal instead of on the problem at hand. As a result, you cannot think logically, your flow of associations dries up and you cannot throw yourself into the problem. When Birch put chimpanzees to solving problems that would bring them bananas, he found that a chimpanzee with a full stomach made no real effort to get to the bananas, while a chimpanzee that had not eaten for a very long time kept repeating the same wrong technique over and over again. It could not break out of its set.

Some of the damage that comes from intense motivation can be avoided if, after you have studied the problem carefully, you put it aside. Then the problem enters an incubation period, where your set can change and your associational thinking can take over. When the writer uses sleep to solve his writing problems, he is making deliberate use of the incubation period. C. Patrick studied a group of poets and artists and found that over 70 percent of them used incubation to solve problems that came up in their work.

Some persons solve crossword puzzles almost as fast as they can write, or they win at Scrabble every time they play. But the person who always loses at Scrabble may be able to fix an ailing motor or figure out a way to make water run uphill while the Scrabble player stands and scratches his head. Different problems demand different skills, different experiences, and different training.

Most psychologists who have worked on problem-solving have made their studies while investigating *intelligence. The American Heritage School Dictionary* calls intelligence "the capacity to learn, think, understand, and know; mental ability." Few persons would argue with that definition, but psychologists are beginning to doubt that such a thing as general intelligence exists, and even more psychologists firmly believe that what passes for an intelligence test does not measure intelligence at all.

It was in France that the intelligence test was born; Alfred Binet began developing a test in 1904. In 1916 the test came across the ocean to Stanford University. There Lewis Terman developed the Stanford-Binet intelligence test, which assumed that the tester was looking for a single ability called intelligence. After you took the test, the tester would add up your score, which represented your *mental age*. He divided this number by your actual or *chronological age*. The answer, multiplied by 100, gave your *intelligence quotient,* which we call IQ.

IQ testing spread through American society and psychologists developed all kinds of IQ tests. Every soldier got an IQ test when he entered the army; every school child got regular tests at school. The results of those IQ tests followed a child from the first grade until he graduated from college. Teachers knew from the tests which children were likely to learn reading and arithmetic without difficulty. IQ tests told counselors which high-school students should take college-preparatory courses. It seemed to work. The first-graders picked out by the test to be good readers usually read well, and most of the students selected as college prospects succeeded at college. IQ tests could predict school performance.

But over the years researchers began to find fault with the idea of general intelligence. First a psychologist suggested that there are two kinds of intelligence; then another said, no, there are seven kinds. Finally a third psychologist said that he could find 120 separate factors that make up what we call intelligence.

Other researchers discovered that an IQ test that worked reasonably well in the United States failed miserably at testing children in Taiwan or India or Venezuela. In Ceylon, for example, university students scored much higher than U.S. university students on the part of the IQ test that measures vocabulary and reading. But they scored much lower on the parts that have nothing to do with language.

Raymond Cattell, who believed in two kinds of intelligence, tried to put together a test that would give similar scores to children from any country. He called it a culture-fair test. It worked for the United States, England, Germany, France,

Italy, and Taiwan, but showed general differences in other parts of the world. When the culture-fair test was developed, the Mensa Society — whose members must have an extremely high IQ — found that three out of every four members picked by the culture-fair test for membership failed the standard intelligence test, and three out of every four members picked by the standard intelligence test failed the culture-fair test.

Only in the past few years have psychologists and sociologists begun to put together solid evidence that IQ tests do not measure intelligence. They measure a person's behavior on a particular kind of problem and predict fairly well how that person will do on other problems of the same kind. Since the tests measure things like vocabulary and arithmetic and reading, they predict how he will do on future vocabulary, arithmetic, and reading-related problems.

A test score cannot tell the tester what caused the behavior it measures. Today, more and more psychologists believe that environment is responsible for much of the confusion over IQ scores. Poor children often make low scores on the tests, and psychologists point out that from the day poor children are born, they have less opportunity to do the things that middle-class children do. They are less likely to visit the zoo or the museum, to travel across the country on vacations, or to have books and records. They get few of the experiences that the people who write textbooks and plan classes assume that all children have. And they get little of the educational push that comes when parents want their children to go to college and stress formal education from the cradle.

The television program "Sesame Street" tries to close some of this gap between privileged and underprivileged children by bringing into the home experiences and knowledge that upper-middle-class children normally have. The Head Start program has the same goal. But sending a child from the subculture of poverty into a single eight-week summer program is like giving a starving man a single steak dinner. One meal will not heal his body, and one short summer session cannot overcome five years of deprivation. The earlier a child's surroundings improve, the closer he will come to catching up with other children.

Animal experiments confirm the importance of one's early environment. David Krech, Mark Rosenzweig, and E. L. Bennett placed baby rats in deprived circumstances. Each rat grew up alone in a small cage, where it could hear little noise. The experimenters handled these rats only when absolutely necessary. Other rats from the same litter grew up in a rich environment. They lived in large cages; they had other rats for companions; they had ladders to climb, tunnels to roam, and wheels to spin. The experimenters often took these rats from their cages and let them explore new territory. Later, both groups of rats had to run mazes and solve simple problems. In every experiment, the rats from the rich environment learned more and learned it faster than the rats from the deprived environment.

The defects of intelligence tests do not mean that there are no differences in intelligence. People are not alike, and different people have different capacities to learn, to think, and to create. Human beings range from persons so retarded that they must be fed, bathed, dressed, and diapered all their lives to towering geniuses like Albert Einstein. Each person probably has a capacity (an intelligence or 120 intelligences) that he cannot exceed, no matter how rich his experience. But most of us never develop to the limits of our capacities.

Intelligence tests are not useless instruments; they do detect deficiencies in experience that can keep a person from succeeding in the regular classroom. They can also detect the person of high capacity and wide experience who is failing in school for reasons that have nothing to do with intelligence. The important thing to remember is that intelligence tests do not measure intelligence — they measure what we have learned from our environment.

Language

8

HUMAN BEINGS TALK to each other. Not all human societies have written languages, but all peoples communicate with words. Anyone who has watched animals knows that they communicate, too. Your dog gives a particular short bark to tell you that he wants to go outdoors. Parrots and parakeets learn to say hello, to curse, or to ask for a cracker. The father quail, on guard while his family forages for food, sounds a warning when he senses danger. One bee dances on the floor of the hive and tells the rest of the bees where to find the pollen-laden flowers.

Some people have said that it is not the production of words that distinguishes man from animals, but the ability to form concepts — to know that a carrot, a radish, a string bean, an ear of corn, and a stalk of asparagus are all vegetables, while an apple — whether red, green, or yellow — an orange, a pear, and a plum are all fruits. But psychologists have taught rats to earn their dinners by choosing triangles from among other geometric shapes, whether the triangles were small or large. And other psychologists have taught pigeons to recognize a human figure in photographs, whether the figure was naked or clothed, standing, lying, peering from behind a tree, on a porch, or sitting in a car.

Man has often tried to teach animals to speak. With the

backing of the United States government, biophysicist John Lilly set up an institute in the Virgin Islands where men could try to talk to dolphins. While the dolphins did learn a few words, the project was not a success. Yet Lilly remains convinced that dolphins have all the intelligence needed to learn English.

Nearly fifty years ago, a professor of psychology at Indiana University took a seven-month old chimpanzee to bring up along with his ten-month old son. Winthrop Kellogg and his wife treated Gua, the female chimpanzee, as if she were a human baby. Although the Kelloggs worked hard with Gua, she did not learn to say a single word. When she was sixteen months old, they gave up and returned her to the Florida primate station that had supplied her.

The Kelloggs quit too soon. Twenty years later, a research psychologist and his wife adopted a three-day old chimpanzee. Cathy and Keith Hayes had no children of their own, so Cathy Hayes gave Viki all her attention. By the time Viki was three years old, she could say — and use at the right times — "Mama," "Papa," and "cup." But Viki never learned a fourth word.

Psychologists Beatrice and Allen Gardner believed that chimpanzees are intelligent enough to talk, but that their vocal apparatus is not flexible enough to shape the sounds of human speech. They decided that if chimpanzees could learn to speak, Viki's vocabulary would not have ended with three words.

But sounds are not the only way to communicate. Deaf persons talk rapidly and fluently in American Sign Language, a language of gestures and finger signs. The Gardners decided that Sign was the ideal way to teach a chimpanzee to talk, and they got a young female chimpanzee to work with. Washoe was born in the wild, so the Gardners were never quite certain of her exact age, but she was between eight and fourteen months old in 1966, when she came to the University of Nevada laboratory.

At least one person was with Washoe whenever she was awake, and that person always used Sign to talk with her. Speaking a language was forbidden, but Washoe's world was not a silent one. Laughing, whistling, or any sound without meaning was permitted.

Washoe did many of the things that children do. After she had been with the Gardners for two months, for example, she had dolls to play with, and in less than a year she was bathing her dolls — soaping, rinsing, and drying them, just as the Gardners bathed her.

Within fifteen months, Washoe knew eighteen signs. She used these signs alone and in combination. Her first sign meant either "come" or "give me," and she soon added "more," "up," "sweet," "open," "tickle," and "go." By twenty-two months, Washoe's vocabulary had increased to thirty-four signs. She would ask for her toothbrush after meals, demand to be tickled, answer questions, and — with rapidly moving hands — sign things like, "You me go out, please," or, when she wanted more food, "Please come give me hurry more."

The Gardners felt that as Washoe grew, she would need the company of other chimpanzees. To keep her from becoming lonely, in 1971 they sent her to live with William B. Lemmon's chimpanzees at the University of Oklahoma. After six years of training, Washoe knows 160 signs, and she knows them well. Once, when an airplane flew over, she looked up and signed, "You me ride in plane."

A few years after the Gardners began to work with Washoe, another psychologist decided to teach a silent language to a chimpanzee. David Premack began teaching Sarah, a five-year old female chimpanzee, to talk using brightly colored plastic tokens. Premack and his team at the University of California made up a number of plastic tokens of different sizes, shapes, and colors, each backed with metal so that it would stick to a magnetized slate.

After Sarah got used to the Santa Barbara laboratory, her trainers established a routine. They would put a banana on the table in front of the chimp and watch while she ate it. Then one day the trainer placed the banana out of Sarah's reach and put before her a small, pink square of plastic. Before Sarah could have her banana, she had to place the square of plastic on the language board.

Being a bright chimpanzee, Sarah quickly learned that the pink square meant "banana." Next she learned that a purple triangle meant "apple." Now the trainers put an apple just out of reach and placed both the square and the triangle before Sarah. She got no fruit until she put the correct plastic token on the language board.

Sarah was ready to learn other words: to learn which plastic token stood for each of her trainers. Sarah's task doubled. The fruit stayed on the far side of the table until two tokens were on the language board: the token that signified which of the trainers — Mary, Debbie, Randy or Jim — was present and the token that represented the piece of fruit.

Token by token, Sarah's vocabulary increased. To get a snack, she had to write, "Debbie give cookie Sarah." She learned to follow directions. When the language board said, "Sarah insert banana pail apple dish," she quickly put the banana into the pail and the apple into the dish.

Sarah's vocabulary grew rapidly. She learned tokens that stood for concepts like same, different, equal, unequal, round, big, and little. She learned colors, prepositions, verbs, and nouns. Within two years, Sarah knew more than 120 words.

But the success of Sarah and of Washoe should not make us believe that, if tomorrow chimpanzees suddenly developed the physical equipment to produce the sounds of English or French or German, there would be no difference between the language of chimpanzees and the language of people. A highly educated person can use and understand about 200,000 words. The average child of three and a half knows more than 1200 words. What's more, even a small child can combine and recombine the words he knows to generate an almost unending string of sentences. And the child learns language easily, while the chimpanzee learns only through intensive training in a carefully planned program. Work with animals shows us that language in animals and in human beings is not something entirely different, but that human language is a highly complex development of a simple animal ability.

There are thousands of languages in the world, and people who grow up learning English have difficulty pronouncing some of the sounds in French or in German and find the clicks of the African Xosa language virtually impossible. When a child is born, it has the ability to learn any language. Charles Osgood recorded all the sounds a baby makes during its first year. He discovered that his tapes contained every possible sound — from the French trill to the Xosan click.

Some psychologists believe that babies learn language just as pigeons learn to peck keys for their dinner. When a baby makes a sound that resembles a word, his parents reinforce him — with smiles, with hugs, by repeating the sound in its correct form, or by reacting appropriately to the word that the sound resembles.

Soon the baby learns to connect the sound with the object

or the action. If he says "Da-Da" when his father is present, Daddy reinforces him; if he says "Da-Da" when his father is out of the room, there is little response. Gradually, "Da-Da" becomes "Daddy." If the sound he makes resembles "more," he gets another cookie.

Sounds — like the Xosan click — that are not part of the language get no reinforcement. Gradually they disappear from the child's vocabulary. Learning language, say behaviorists like B. F. Skinner, is a matter of "shaping verbal behavior."

Many linguists and other psychologists say that this explanation cannot account for all language learning. They agree that reinforcement plays an important role, especially in teaching a child the vocabulary of his native language. But they insist that knowing the names of things and of actions is a small part of speaking a language.

The structure of a language is complex, says linguist Noam Chomsky, and a toddler could never discover the ways that words fit together to form sentences from the parent who shapes his verbal behavior with cookies and kisses.

Persons who support Chomsky's view of language learning say that all languages in the world — no matter how different they sound — have the same deep structure. The ability to learn a language, so the argument goes, is somehow wired into the human being. Each baby's mind is set in a predetermined way so that, as he reaches the age of eighteen months or so and begins to put two words together, he naturally processes those words according to the rules of the universal deep structure.

We might call this structure the rules of a grammar, an inborn grammar that makes a child accept a string of words like "the spotted dog barked loudly" as a sentence but reject "barked spotted loudly dog the" as nonsense. The baby does not learn this structure; it develops as he grows, just as the ability to walk develops. All the baby needs to develop this ability is to be in a place where he hears a spoken language.

Psychologists and linguists are working hard to discover which of these theories is best, and the disagreement is deep. Psychologist D. O. Hebb has suggested a middle view. A child is born, he says, with the ability to analyze the sounds he hears and to learn the meaning of these sounds and of gestures. With these and other inborn abilities, the child learns the structure of the language as well as the words.

But Hebb disagrees with behaviorists who assume that all language learning is on the pigeon or rat level of simple operant conditioning. More complicated forms, such as latent learning, play a major role in all language learning — in the learning of both structure and vocabulary.

All the words that make up the vocabulary of a language carry two kinds of meaning. One meaning is *denotative;* this meaning is "what the word points to," the thing or things to which a word applies. All users of the language should agree on the denotative meaning of a word.

The second meaning is *connotative;* this meaning includes all the associations and emotional implications of a word. A word may have different connotative meanings for different people, or the same connotative meanings may be accepted by most. For example, a Democrat is a person who is a registered member of the Democratic party. That is the denotative meaning of the word. But a Democrat's connotative meanings for *Democrat* are very different from the meanings a Republican attaches to the word.

Such disagreements can be serious. Connotative meanings have built one of the barriers that stand in the way of world peace. The different meanings that different peoples attach to words keep them from communicating. As long as different countries mean different things when they talk about democracy, freedom, aggression, liberation, peace, and socialism, the prospects for a harmonious world are dim.

If language teaches an Arab to notice camels and their trappings and an American to notice cars and their accessories, perhaps it has an even more powerful influence on growing members of the culture. Benjamin Lee Whorf thought so, and so do some other linguists, psychologists, and anthropologists. Whorf believed that a person's native language shapes the way he looks at the world.

Languages talk about the world in different ways. If you want your dinner, you say, "I am hungry," and a Frenchman or a Mexican says, "I have hunger." But if a Navajo's dinner is late, he says, "Hunger is killing me." In the Navajo language, hunger is not a feeling that comes from within — a system out of homeostasis. An outside force, one that man cannot hope to control, makes a person hungry.

Navajos and Anglos look at the world of nature differently. The Navajo feels he cannot master nature; all he can hope to do is use what nature provides and try to influence nature with song and ritual. The Anglo sees nature as a force to be controlled; he tries to bend nature to his will. If the Navajo's farm is flooded, he moves; the Anglo builds a dam. The Navajo lives with nature without changing its face; the Anglo bulldozes hills for housing projects and tunnels through tall mountains to build roads.

Whorf believed that language itself causes these different ways of living in the world. While many would argue that this theory gives language a power it does not have, it is plain that languages talk about the world in different ways and reveal what a culture feels its members should notice and consider important.

Speech is not the only way human beings communicate. Suppose you are speaking to someone you dislike. Your words are polite, but the message you send along with those words probably tells the other person that you are not friendly. The tone of your voice, the expression on your face, the gestures you make, the way you hold your body, the distance between the two of you, and the amount of time you spend looking into the other person's eyes, all signal your feelings and betray your words.

After studying people under all sorts of conditions, Albert Mehrabian estimated that only 7 percent of the information you give other people comes from your words. They get another 38 percent from your tone of voice and rely upon your facial expression and your body for 55 percent of your message.

Suppose your friend is coming up the steps, holding an ice-cream cone in each hand. He stumbles and sprawls across the porch, and the ice cream lands on the floor. As he picks himself up, unhurt but embarrassed, you say, "You're as graceful as a gazelle." Your words are complimentary, but the acid tone of your voice and the disappointment in your face tell him that you think he's perhaps the clumsiest person in the universe. If you had put up the money for the ice cream, the acid would have been stronger and the message twice as clear.

If, on the other hand, your comment had come just after your friend had won the song-and-dance lead in the school production of *South Pacific*, your voice and face would have strengthened your words, telling your friend that you respected his agility and dancing skill.

Mehrabian applied electronics to people's voices and found that we convey our messages even when others do not know what we are saying. When his electronic filter suppressed the higher frequencies in recorded speech, listeners could not distinguish one word from another. But they had no trouble at all telling how much the speaker liked or disliked the person he or she was talking to.

Next Mehrabian taped other messages. In some of them the speaker made a complimentary remark, but used a negative tone of voice, as when you told your clumsy friend that he was as graceful as a gazelle. In other messages the words and the tone of voice agreed, and in the rest, an insult was delivered in friendly tones. Mehrabian presented these messages to three different groups and asked them to tell whether the speaker liked or disliked the person he was talking to. One group read a written transcription of the words, the second heard the taped messages distorted by the electronic filter, and the third heard the tape directly, so that both the words and the tone were plain.

Those who read the message reported it as friendly when the words were kind and said it was unfriendly when the words were hostile. The second group's judgment agreed with the tone of the distorted tape. The third group, which heard the entire message, found the kind messages friendlier when the tone and words agreed and the unfriendly messages more hostile. But when the words and the tone contradicted each other, the tone won every time. The listeners judged the meaning of the message by the tone — not the words.

Smiles, frowns, raised eyebrows, nose-scratching, ear-tugging, and hair-twisting are other messages we send along with our words. Our eyes can express boredom, anger, hatred, compassion, liking, or love. When we like a person, we tend to look into his eyes when we speak to him. Mehrabian suspects that our distrust of people with "shifty eyes" comes not because they tend to change the direction of their glances, but because they avoid giving us the signal "I like you" that direct eye contact conveys.

Our posture reveals more than we intend it should. A rigid body may send a message of dislike, a relaxed body, a message of friendship. The more we like someone, the closer we lean toward him in conversation.

Many of these body signals are different in different cultures — or even subcultures. When researchers studied university students, they found that Arab students stood closer to each other, touched each other more, looked more into each other's eyes, and talked louder than American students did. K. B. Little asked persons from five different cultures to arrange dolls to show different social situations — friends meeting, couples dating, and the like. He found that Greeks placed the dolls closest together, Americans put them a little farther apart, Italians put more space between their dolls than Americans did, Swedes placed their dolls even farther apart, and Scots put more distance between their dolls than any other group. J. C. Baxter studied people who visited a zoo. He found that when a pair toured the zoo, Chicanos stood closest together, Anglos took a middle position, and blacks stood farthest from their companions.

When we consider human speech, we must always remember that the words that issue from our lips are only part of the signals we constantly send others. We can say what we mean, or we can say more than we mean, or we can say less than we mean. Unfortunately — and this is perhaps the most important point — we can say what we don't mean, and mask the tone and facial expression that would reveal the lie. It may be that the human ability to give false information, and to give it intentionally, is a major difference between animal and human communication.

Personality

9

I̲ᴛ ɪꜱ ᴘʟᴀɪɴ that no two persons are exactly alike. Some people are at ease in crowds, meet strangers easily, and often lead clubs or committees. Others prefer to be alone, are uneasy with strangers, and never speak up in groups. Given a free hour, one person will read; another will watch television or go for a swim or write a letter or work on a model or arrange a stamp collection or tune a car engine or weed a flower bed. Still others cannot be comfortable by themselves and will go to great lengths to find companions.

When a psychologist explains emotions or motivation or learning, he talks about human beings as if all persons behaved the same way in the same situation. But psychologists know better than anyone that people are not alike. In every experiment, some subjects behave in an unusual manner. When a psychologist reports, for example, that most air-force men are afraid in combat, he means that while 86 percent say they are afraid, 14 percent say they feel *no* fear.

When we turn to the individual, the single person who may or may not behave as the psychologist predicts, we are beginning to study personality. To an individual, his personality is himself — "the real Me." But when we talk about personality, we are still talking about behavior. Others judge an individual's personality by putting together his behavior over a long period of time in many situations. From what he does they form an idea about him and about the ways he is likely to behave in the future. They may say, "John is serious, quiet, and determined. He is shy, but kind."

Psychologists have put forth many different theories of personality. William H. Sheldon, a physician and psychologist, developed a theory of personality based upon body build. He believed that there are three different body types: *endomorphs,* who are soft and fat; *mesomorphs,* who are strong and muscular; and *ectomorphs,* who are tall and thin. If one were to draw a geometric figure that resembled each body type, he would draw a circle for the endomorph, a triangle standing on its point for the mesomorph, and a vertical line for the ectomorph.

Next Sheldon examined personality. He studied 33 young men for a whole year, after rating them for body types. At the end of the year, he came up with three personality types to match the three body types. Endomorphs, he said, are likely to love comfort, to be sociable, greedy, relaxed, slow to react, tolerant, and to have even tempers. Mesomorphs are aggressive, courageous, move about a great deal, and dominate others. Ectomorphs are restrained, inhibited, secretive, self-conscious, react quickly, fear other people, and like to be alone.

Sheldon had a theory as to why persons with similar builds have similar personalities. Personality might come along with the genes, he speculated. If one can inherit a tall body or a particular kind of muscle structure, one might also inherit the temperament that goes along with the bones and muscles. But nurture could be more important than nature, he admitted. One's environment could form one's personality. A baby who is stuffed by its mother has a good chance of being fat, gluttonous, and lazy. A child who is encouraged to run, jump, swim and play baseball is likely to develop strong muscles and to act aggressively.

The environment can work in other ways, too, Sheldon noted. Culture exerts a powerful influence on its members. If a culture expects a fat person to be good-natured and easygoing, and a very thin person to be self-conscious and inhibited, individuals are likely to behave in just that way. Positive reinforcement also shapes behavior. A fat person is not likely to be rewarded when he tries out for the track team, and a thin, frail person may fail when he tries to dominate others.

Not everyone fits neatly into one of Sheldon's three body types. Most of us have physiques that are a mixture of the three types.

Sheldon's work has been attacked by other researchers, who have pointed out that his experiments relied more on his own theories than on measured data and that his personality types were closer to physical descriptions than to psychological ones.

But recent research has supported some of Sheldon's findings. Juan B. Cortés and Florence M. Gatti studied college students, prison inmates, and both delinquent and nondelinquent teen-age boys. They carefully measured each subject's body to determine his type and gave a series of detailed personality tests. They found that personalities and body types were closely related. They also discovered that the group of convicts had three times as many mesomorphs as the group of college students. The mesomorphs they studied also showed a strong need for achievement, while the ectomorphs showed less than a normal need to succeed.

Another way to divide people into personality types is to label them as *extraverts* or *introverts*. Carl G. Jung, one of the founders of psychoanalysis, developed this method of classifying personalities. An extravert is the outgoing person who quickly responds to the world around him; an introvert is the quiet, withdrawn person who is concerned with his own thoughts and feelings.

Jung's terms have become part of popular language, and people readily classify themselves and others as introverts or extraverts. But extraverts and introverts are extreme types, and most of us do not fit comfortably in either category. Jung would classify us as *ambiverts*, persons whose personalities hover somewhere between the two extremes and who have some characteristics of each type.

Julian Rotter's method of classifying persons again divides people into two groups: those who believe they control their own actions and those who believe that fate or powerful persons control them. Rotter calls those who believe that they have freedom of action, who think that their actions influence the world about them, *internally controlled*. He calls those who believe that luck or chance determines their actions, who think that what they do has no effect on the world about them, *externally controlled*.

Internals tend to be nonsmokers, or, if they do smoke, find it possible to quit. They tend to be active in political or social movements; they can make other people change their minds; and they refuse to cooperate when they think other people are trying to manipulate them.

Externals find it difficult, if not impossible, to stop smoking. They may go to a political rally, but they are not likely to work actively in a movement. They are not very successful in persuading others to change their minds; they are less likely than internals to resist when they think others are trying to manipulate them. Because they believe others manipulate them, externals are suspicious of authority. This makes them likely to believe that the Warren Commission Report of President Kennedy's assassination covered up a conspiracy.

Again, externals and internals describe two ends of a scale. Most persons fall somewhere between the two extremes.

A fourth way to classify personality was developed at the close of World War II. A group of researchers wanted to find out why the German people followed Adolf Hitler and supported his campaign against the Jews — a policy which sent six million European Jews to their deaths. After the war, T. W. Adorno, Elsa Frenkel-Brunswik, D. J. Levinson, and Nevitt Sanford interviewed many persons, looking for the personality characteristics that might explain Hitler's success.

When they found the characteristics of the *anti-Semite* — the person who dislikes Jews — they discovered that they were actually studying the *authoritarian* personality type. On the basis of their research, they developed the California-F scale (F stands for facism), a test that measures authoritarianism.

The authoritarian person, they said, wants to live a tough and manly life; he is superstitious and tends to believe in astrology; he accepts without question the rules of conduct set forth by his society; he wants to punish severely anyone who breaks those rules of conduct, especially the rules about sex; he is afraid of genuine feelings or of thinking about the reasons behind a person's actions; and he believes that man is naturally evil. Because of these tendencies, the authoritarian personality needs to submit to a strong leader, and he is suspicious of psychotherapy and psychology.

If the work of Adorno and his colleagues was accurate, it still did not explain why so many Germans were ready to embrace fascism in the 1920s and 1930s. Recently Stephen Sales, who was a psychologist at Carnegie-Mellon University, decided to find out why. Sales had been a historian before he became a psychologist, and his studies had convinced him that when a person feels threatened, he becomes more authoritarian. Sales believed that the defeat of Germany in World War I, followed by economic chaos and weak government, had left the German people threatened and ripe for Hitler's appeals.

If this was so, he said, authoritarianism will rise in hard times and lose influence in good times. Sure enough, when he checked church membership in the United States between 1920 and 1939, he found that when jobs were scarce and people had little money, they tended to join very strict churches — those that demanded obedience. In the years when people had more money, they seemed to join churches that allowed their members to make up their own minds about most issues.

As Sales looked more closely at the United States, he found that during times of economic hardship the mark of the authoritarian personality showed in many places. When people had little money, red-blooded magazines that stressed masculine power sold well, astrology became popular, books and articles on psychotherapy began to disappear, police budgets increased even when there was less crime, rapists got longer prison terms, and more people had to sign loyalty oaths. New comic strips were likely to be about powerful characters like Superman. (In good times, a new comic strip is likely to be about a family, such as Gasoline Alley.)

If Sales's interpretations are right, then a country should have little to fear from fascism during times of prosperity. But widespread depression or other events that make the citizens feel insecure will also make them responsive to the appeals of fascism.

Theories of personality that divide people into *types* are generally unsatisfactory. They try to explain a person's behavior with too little information. And a person will fit into one of the categories only if we ignore other parts of his personality. The person we classify as an introvert may surprise us by having a good time at a party; the person we consider an internal may turn out to be a chain smoker.

Psychologists continue to search for more precise ways to describe personality. Some have developed theories that divide an individual's personality into a number of *traits*. By rating a person on many traits, these psychologists believe that they can give a more accurate picture of personality.

One of the leading advocates of the trait theory of personality is Raymond B. Cattell. He has developed a mathematical approach to personality that produces scores on sixteen different personality traits such as friendliness, sensitivity, realism, and modesty. Cattell has shown that happily married couples score the same on most traits, but usually make different scores on a particular trait — dominance, the tendency to want to control a situation. Couples that break up, he has shown, tend to have different scores on several important traits, but similar scores on dominance. The importance of the dominance trait is obvious. If both persons want to control a situation, a clash is inevitable, while if one person wants to control and the other would rather be controlled, no problem will arise.

An approach like Cattell's describes a person better than a type theory does. While two people may score the same on a trait or two, each person's pattern of sixteen scores will be unique, just as his fingerprints are unique.

Psychoanalysis looks at personality in yet another way. Sigmund Freud developed a theory that sees personality developing from the action between one's instincts and the restrictions of one's environment. He divided the personality into the *id*, the *ego*, and the *superego*. Freud placed all the primitive instincts in the id. The ego tries to regulate the impulses of the id, so that the person can keep the respect of himself and of society. The superego is the conscience; it holds the standards of right and wrong that the person learned in childhood. As an individual grows from a baby to an adult, his own personality comes from the way his id, ego, and superego act together or in opposition to solve the problems of each stage of development.

Freud never tested his theories by running experiments in a laboratory. His ideas of personality developed from his own experiences and his contact with his patients. But two psychologists who are very much at home in a laboratory adopted Freud's basic theory and used the behaviorist's principles of stimulus and response to explain it. John Dollard and Neal Miller talked about the id, the ego, and the superego in terms that behaviorist John B. Watson would find familiar.

Their explanation stressed *learning* and came from laboratory studies of learning and motivation. Dollard and Miller believed that the rewards and punishments that follow a person's actions form his personality. And they saw those actions as a person's attempts to reduce his biological drives by seeking pleasure and avoiding pain. Some of those drives are hunger, thirst, sex, and pain.

Behaviorists like Dollard and Miller would object to trait theories of personality as inaccurate. They would point out that a trait is only a term that describes a lot of separate behavior. The behavior that we bundle together and call a trait has many causes and is difficult to study in the laboratory. They would rather study single responses, which are easier to label and to measure.

Still other theorists believe that the learning approach of

Dollard and Miller is far too simple. The humanistic psychologists reject both the behaviorist's description of personality and the theories of psychoanalysis. Their ideas of personality might best be called *self* theories.

Carl Rogers believes that two systems regulate a person's behavior: the total *organism,* which is the whole individual, and the *self,* which is the conscious part of one's being — what one considers "I" or "me." The eyes and ears and nose and internal organs and nerve endings of the organism receive a constant barrage of stimulation from the sights and sounds and objects in the world and from its bodily processes and the movements of its muscles.

A newborn baby girl has no self, for she cannot distinguish herself from the world around her. As the baby grows, her self develops. She learns the difference between "me" and "mother" and "milk" and "blanket." As the child sees the results of her actions on the world around her, she develops her concept of her self. She finds that she likes some of the things her self does and dislikes others.

The organism maintains itself by responding to drives, and it tries to *actualize* itself. Rogers explains actualizing as the organism's attempts to improve and to grow and to become independent.

The self and the organism can work together or they can refuse to cooperate. If they work together, the person likes herself and others and is open to experience. If the organism keeps information away from the self, or if the self denies the organism's actions, the person may be headed for trouble. She may become disturbed and unhappy.

The idea of actualization was developed further by Abraham Maslow. Maslow believed that psychologists spend too much time studying sick people. His theories of personality came from studying healthy persons. Maslow believed that the human being has many needs that range from simple ones like hunger and affection to exalted needs like justice, goodness, and beauty. But he believed that the simple needs must be fulfilled before a person can feel or act upon the higher needs. The higher needs are always there, even if a person is not aware of them. If they are not fulfilled, a person may become mentally ill.

Maslow called someone whose life fulfills all his higher needs a *self-actualized* person. He pointed out that not many people ever become self-actualized, but he listed some who had: Abraham Lincoln, Ludwig van Beethoven, Albert Einstein, Henry David Thoreau, and Eleanor Roosevelt.

Nothing in this chapter has told you the things you wanted to find out when you began it: why some people are popular; why some of the people you know like you while others do not; why you like the girl who lives two houses away from you but can't stand the boy who lives across the street. That's something you can't learn from studying a psychologist's theory of personality.

But psychologists have studied the ways people behave together. From their work you can get a pretty good idea about the effects you have on others. People form a picture of your personality not just from what you say, but on the basis of how you look and how you behave. Perhaps your clothes proclaim that you follow the latest fads, or perhaps they tell others that fashion makes no difference to you or even that you reject the whole idea of fashion. You may be well-groomed, or you may be sloppy. Your hair may be cut short, or it may fall down your back, or it may be piled high on your head.

The first impression you make with your appearance can change as soon as you begin to speak or to act — not so much from what you say as from the tone in which you say it. All the elements of silent communication — posture, gestures, expression, eye contact, how close you stand — help mold the picture of personality that you project.

As soon as you lean forward, speak, walk across the room, or hand someone a book, others are combining what they see and hear into a general picture. Most of us are not aware of the ways in which we form these impressions, or even that the process is going on. But if asked about someone we have met only a few times, we find we can say, "He's friendly," or, "She's a showoff."

Dennis Krebs says that when we form a picture of someone's personality, we generally go through three stages. First we notice a person's behavior and decide that he is happy or tired or nervous or sad. We make a judgment about his present emotional state. If we see that person several times and each time we meet he is in the same emotional state, we decide that the state is not his emotional response to a recent event, but a personality trait. The person must generally be happy or nervous or sad. When we have detected several personality traits in the same person — nervousness, shyness, aloofness, quietness — we combine them into a personality *type*. We decide that the person is an introvert or "a mouse" or "stuck-up," depending upon how we interpret that combination of traits.

We also bring our own opinions and prejudices to personality judging. The ways in which we expect others to behave often play as great a part in our ideas of their personalities as the ways in which they actually behave. If we believe that people with skin of a certain color or people who belong to a certain religion or whose parents come from a particular country will behave alike, their actual behavior and personalities will have little effect on our pictures of them. We will expect the tone-deaf ectomorph — if his skin is black — to excel at music and football.

Not all our personality preconceptions are based on racial or religious prejudice. We also tend to find whatever traits we look for in most people we meet. S. M. Dornbusch tested the way in which children judge personality. He asked a group of ten- and eleven-year-olds who had attended the same summer camp to describe their tentmates. When two children described the same person, 45 percent of the personality traits they listed were the same, but 55 percent were different. This suggests that a child's own behavior and personality accounted for less than half the picture his tentmates had formed of him. When one child described two persons, 57 percent of the personality traits he listed were the same. If he expected to find friendly or kind or honest persons, he found them. But if he expected to find unfriendly or selfish or dishonest children at camp, apparently he found them instead.

Part of the error in personality judging by summer-camp children may not have been in the judges themselves. No one presents his naked self to the world. Each of us has a number of faces. With some people, we are serious; with others we are light-hearted and avoid important issues; the person our parents know is a different person from the one our close friends know or the person our teachers know.

In spite of the different people we are, we never feel that we are dishonest when we present our different faces. And we are not. The behavior and appearance of others can change the opinions we have of ourselves.

Stanley J. Morse and Kenneth Gergen asked male students at the University of Michigan to apply for a summer job. When each applicant came into the room, they gave him a stack of tests to fill out and left him alone at a long table.

Among the tests he had to complete was a self-evaluation questionnaire.

While the student was taking his tests, another person entered the room. Half of the students saw a neat, clean, well-groomed man. He wore a good suit, his shoes shone, and he carried an attaché case. When he sat down to wait, he took out a dozen sharpened pencils and a book of philosophy. The person the rest of the students saw was a mess. He wore a torn, dirty sweatshirt and grimy Levi's cut off at the knees. He needed a shave, and in his hand was a popular, sexy novel. Neither man spoke to the student who was taking the tests.

When Morse and Gergen scored the self-evaluation tests, they found that the self-esteem of students who were in the room with the well-groomed person dropped sharply. They felt sloppy and stupid in comparison to him. But the self-esteem of students who were in the room with the sloppy person zoomed upward. The slob made them feel neat and intelligent.

Sometimes we make a deliberate change in our behavior and it will change the way in which we think of ourselves. Gergen asked a woman to interview 18 female students. Before each interview, he took the student aside and asked her to help him out by making the interviewer like her. She could do or say anything she wished. Every student talked about herself as if she were describing a combination of Madame Curie and Ali McGraw. She was popular, sensitive, industrious, and clever.

After the meeting with the interviewer, each student took a private, self-rating test. When Gergen compared these tests with tests the same students had taken a month before, he found that their self-esteem had shot upward.

Students in a control group, who had not been asked to

make the interviewer like them, gave modest descriptions of themselves. Their scores on the self-rating tests after the interviews showed no change from their earlier scores.

This and other studies have convinced Gergen that people can improve the pictures they have of themselves just by thinking of their good qualities. Apparently none of us has a single, rigid personality.

For years, psychologists have said that a healthy person has a stable personality, one that remains generally the same over a long period of time. But that personality has many facets and it continues to grow and to change. Time and experience can change motivations, habits, and behavior.

Any personality theory is useful if one does not try to fit a single personality inside it and snip off whatever refuses to fit the mold just as Cinderella's stepsisters chopped at their feet to make them fit the glass slipper. None of the theories satisfies all psychologists, but each gives us a glimpse of the ways that personality works and each helps us to understand human nature.

Adjustment

10

No ONE GETS what he wants all of the time. Sometimes you strive for a goal and fail. A small college refuses to admit you; the coach says you're too slow for the football team; the girl or boy who attracts you acts as if you didn't exist. Life often frustrates people, and each person reacts differently to frustration.

There are several kinds of barriers that frustrate our motives and keep us from reaching our goals. One kind of barrier is physical. A baby stretches its arm through the bars of its playpen, but the rattle remains just beyond its grasp. A child's ball bounces over the fence into the yard of a disagreeable neighbor.

Time is another physical barrier. The student cannot vote until he is eighteen, no matter how strongly he feels about an election. The patient with cancer will not know if he is cured until the sixth year after his surgery.

Other barriers are thrown up by society. NASA rejects a woman's application to join the astronaut program because of her sex; a country club rejects a membership application because of a couple's race or religion; a social clique at school rebuffs the friendly overtures of a new student whose father works in a service station.

Sometimes the barriers to our goals lie within us. A boy

stutters so badly he shuns social engagements; a girl is too fat and clumsy to become a ballerina; a student wants desperately to become a lawyer but lacks the intelligence.

A barrier does not always mean permanent frustration. Faced with an obstacle, a person will sometimes work harder to get to his goal. He will try to solve his problem with greater effort or by using a different method. The child may climb the fence after his ball; the baby may scream until its mother hands it the toy; the boy who stutters may get professional help with his speech.

Sometimes we are faced with opposing goals, and satisfying one means frustrating the other. When we are caught between conflicting motives, we engage in *conflict behavior*. In one kind of conflict, we have a choice of two desirable goals, but to choose one means to lose the other. This is an *approach-approach* conflict. You must choose between going to a Dustin Hoffman movie or a rock concert. Two courses you need for high-school graduation are scheduled for the same period.

The second kind of conflict is the *avoidance-avoidance* conflict. Faced with the draft, a young man may have to choose between fighting in a war he opposes or leaving the country. A student must choose between taking a test he fears he will fail and cutting the class. An adult must choose between certain death and a dangerous operation.

The third kind of conflict is the *approach-avoidance* conflict. The same goal both attracts and repels the person: he would like to be in the school play, but he is so shy that he is afraid to audition for a part. He would like to go swimming but the water is cold. A mother wants her child to grow up, but she doesn't want to lose her dependent baby. Sometimes a person is caught in a *double approach-avoidance* conflict: two goals

lie before him, and each of them has both pleasant and unpleasant aspects.

Often we have little trouble resolving conflict behavior; it's
as easy as deciding which chocolate to choose from a box. If
the movie will be on next week, we go to the rock concert
without a second thought. We close our eyes and jump quickly
into the cold water of the swimming pool.

Research with rats has taught psychologists a lot about how
people in conflict act. Neal Miller constructed a small leather
harness for his rats and attached it, by means of cords and pul-
leys, to a spring that measured the amount of pull exerted by
the rat. When he placed food at the end of a long alley, the
harnessed rat pulled harder and harder as it neared the food.
When Miller placed the rat in an alley where it had earlier received electric shocks, the rat pulled hardest to get away when
it was closest to the spot where it had been shocked. Fear was
stronger than hunger. The hungry rat pulled harder to get
away from the threat of electric shock than it pulled to reach
the food it wanted.

When Miller placed his rats in an approach-approach conflict, they decided quickly. When the rat was placed halfway
between two feeding places, the slightest movement to one
side or the other brought the rat closer to one food source. It
always chose the dinner that had become closer.

In approach-approach conflicts, a slight advantage is all it
takes to make one motive stronger than the other. If two
courses you need are scheduled for the same period, you will
choose the one that appears slightly more attractive to you —
perhaps because you are interested in the subject or because
you like the instructor.

Rats in avoidance-avoidance conflict can become immobi-
lized. When a rat was put in an alley halfway between two

places where it had been shocked, the slightest movement placed it closer to one of the sources of pain and it moved away. If the rat moved past the midpoint, it was again closer to one of the pain sources than the other and so it moved back toward the center again. The only thing that could get the rat off dead center was a chance to escape. If it could climb over the alley wall, it did so. But if there was no way out, the rat remained crouched in the center, afraid to move in either direction. In the same way, the person faced with the choice between possible death and an operation often postpones his decision until he becomes convinced that surgery is his only chance for life and therefore the lesser of the two evils.

A rat found itself in an approach-avoidance conflict when it had been fed and shocked in the same alley. It wanted to move down the alley to reach the food, but it also feared the electric shock that sometimes awaited it. When the rat was some distance away, the pull of the food was stronger than its fear, and it began to move toward the end of the alley. The closer the rat got to the place where it had been both fed and shocked, the stronger its fear became. At last, fear took over and the rat moved back to a place where the pull of the food and the fear of the shock were equal. This kind of conflict made the rat a prisoner, unable to act. It did not want to escape because it was drawn by the food. People in an approach-avoidance conflict often become so trapped by a situation that both attracts and repels them that they develop personality and behavior problems.

We cannot always solve our conflicts, and so we react to frustration in different ways. Anger is the commonest response, and it can lead to aggression, as we saw in Chapter Four.

In a test of frustration, A. F. Zander asked a group of fifth-

and sixth-grade students to memorize long lists of numbers. While the students were studying the numbers, Zander changed the list. Later, when the students were tested, none of the numbers they remembered were on Zander's list. Many of these frustrated children became aggressive, and one boy — who had always been well-behaved — started a fist fight as soon as he left the testing room. Zander became immensely unpopular with the students he tested — even though he never admitted to them that he had switched lists. When he walked through the school corridors, children made faces at him, called him names, and kicked and hit him.

But we don't always respond to frustration with aggression. From the time we are babies, our families, our friends, and the society around us tell us that open aggression is bad. A two-year-old learns that he can't hit his baby sister because she takes Mother away from him and that he can't kick the dog because the rain keeps him inside. Now there is a new conflict — the battle between the child's impulse to express his frustration by hitting and his fear that he will be punished if he hits. That two-year-old may fear a spanking or he may fear being exiled to his room, but he may also fear something that becomes stronger as he grows — his own feelings of guilt that come whenever he does something he has learned is "wrong." He doesn't want to be a "bad boy."

Placed in a frustrating situation, we can avoid the whole thing by withdrawing. Like the person confronted with the choice between death and surgery, we can refuse to choose. But when we withdraw, the situation remains; we have solved nothing. The student who cuts class because he did not write the assigned paper has withdrawn from the frustrating situation, but he must eventually face the teacher and the consequences of his behavior.

The fear that sometimes accompanies frustration can turn into *anxiety*. We feel afraid and helpless but we don't understand why we are afraid; we know only that we can't solve our problems. This anxiety strikes at our self-esteem and we cannot endure it for long. Thrown into a state of anxiety, we stop trying to solve our problems and instead look for a way to get rid of the terrible dread that besets us.

One way to escape is to distort the world around us. We change the way we perceive the world and the problem no longer is a problem — to us. A student convinces himself that in spite of missed assignments and failing test grades, he will pass his algebra course. The F that he finds on his report card surprises no one but himself.

The ways in which we distort reality are called *defense mechanisms*, because they defend us against a truth we cannot bear to face. All of us use some of these defenses at some time because they ease our anxieties, soften our failures, and bolster our self-esteem. But we use them without knowing what we have done; the distortion becomes reality to us.

One way to avoid a problem is to deny that it exists, just as the student denied to himself the obvious fact that he was failing his algebra course. Sometimes a person who discovers that he has advanced cancer uses *denial* to ease his anxieties. He denies the seriousness of his illness and his probable fate. A person may even refuse to talk about an upsetting event because discussing the painful situation would threaten his denial of it. Prisoners in German concentration camps during World War II used denial to defend themselves. They told themselves, "This isn't happening to me," or, "It can't really be true; such things don't happen."

Sometimes we push threatening or painful thoughts out of our consciousness; no matter how hard we try, we cannot remember the event or the situation that terrifies us. Psychologists call this *repression*, and many suspense movies center on the hero's or heroine's attempts to remember a repressed but dangerous event. A soldier who by mistake shoots one of his own company during an enemy attack may suffer such a loss of memory. He becomes nervous, trembles, and can remember neither the battle nor his name. With the use of drugs and therapy, however, psychologists can help him to recall the repressed memory.

In the state psychologists call *isolation*, we accept threatening events or feelings intellectually, but we block out the emotion that normally goes along with the knowledge. We explain away the death of someone close to us by saying, "He lived a full life," or, "She died quickly and didn't have to suffer." The failing student will say, "I should work harder," and the person who never gives to charity may say, "I should be less selfish." In these cases, saying the right words takes away the guilt and allows the person to keep right on failing or being greedy with a clear conscience.

Sometimes we take care of threats and frustrations by adopting a safe, available substitute. A childless woman resolves her frustrations by shifting her affection from the child she cannot have to a pet dog. She fusses over the dog as if it were a baby, watching its diet, its exercise, and its every movement.

This defense mechanism is called *displacement*, and a frustrated person often displaces his aggression, attacking by word or deed someone or something that has no connection with whatever frustrated him. When you find yourself fighting with your brother just after your mother has punished you, you probably have displaced your aggression from your mother to your brother.

Displaced aggression showed up when Neal Miller and R.

Bugelski tested the prejudice of workers in a summer camp. The workers first answered a questionnaire that measured their attitudes toward Mexicans and Japanese. Then Miller and Bugelski set about frustrating them. They made each worker take several long, hard tests that he could not possibly pass. The tests lasted so long that the workers missed the weekly movie. And to make it even worse, they also missed the lottery that was held each week at the theater.

Now the workers filled out the prejudice questionnaire once again. The scores showed that the workers were more hostile toward Mexicans and Japanese than they had been before they were frustrated. They had displaced part of their aggression onto the minority groups.

Displaced aggression can be harmful to its victims. During the period from 1882 to 1930, the price of cotton in the South appeared to affect the number of lynchings. Whenever the price of cotton went down, the number of lynchings went up. Southerners frustrated by the financial hardships caused by low cotton prices apparently took out their frustration on the blacks.

Projection takes place when a person shifts the blame for his own mistakes to someone else. The basketball player who falls down on the court comes back to look for the slippery spot on the floor; the fat person who refuses to admit that he is greedy says that he overeats because other people offer him rich food and drink. We use projection when we blame our failures on fate or on bad luck. In its extreme form, projection can turn into *paranoia,* a disorder in which a person believes that other people are plotting against him or spying on him or even attempting to kill him.

People with strict consciences may project their unacceptable thoughts and feelings onto others. The unmarried woman who believes that her sexual desires are wrong may say that "today's young people are oversexed." Projection allows us to thrust "bad" thoughts out of our minds, thus reducing our anxieties.

We can also distort reality in the opoosite direction by using *identification*. We identify ourselves closely with someone else who has the qualities we would like to have for ourselves. A young boy may identify with Roger Staubach and take the quarterback's triumphs and defeats as if they were his own. He may try to dress, to walk, and to talk like his model. Television commercials that use sport stars to sell hair tonic or shaving cream exploit this tendency in us. Parents often identify with their children and take a child's successes and failures for their own.

Identification is not limited to a single person; one can identify with an entire football team, with a political party, with a club, with one's profession, or with the company one works for. A man who feels unworthy because he is only a mailroom clerk gets a sense of power and worth by identifying himself with Montgomery Ward. And the boy from the ghetto gains strength when he identifies with his local gang.

There is another kind of identification called *introjection*. One identifies with one's persecutors, accepting their beliefs and values, even though they conflict with one's own standards. In this way, one gets some of the power that belongs to the other person or group.

The child who plays dentist after a painful session in the dentist's chair is a mild example of introjection. An extreme form developed in the German concentration camps, when some Jewish prisoners took over the standards of the Gestapo.

They mimicked the guards' anti-Semitic vocabulary, their cruelty, and even tried to make their concentration-camp garb look like Gestapo uniforms.

A frustrated, anxious person does not always distort the world around him when he cannot reach his goal. Sometimes he uses *rationalization* and finds a reason for his failure that he can accept. The most famous rationalizer is the fox in Aesop's fable. When, after many tries, the hungry fox could not reach the hanging cluster of plump, black grapes, he gave up and told himself that he didn't really want the fruit; the grapes probably were sour. Rationalization made the fox's disappointment easier to bear, for who would want a bunch of sour grapes? It also justified his behavior — the fox could give up his quest for the grapes without feeling like a quitter.

When you hear a young man say that a girl who refused him a date probably isn't good company, or when you hear the girl who was admitted to a second-rate college explain the special benefits of the school, you are meeting with rationalization. And when you tell yourself that you got a C instead of a B in chemistry because the teacher disliked you, you are propping up your own self-esteem with rationalization.

We search desperately for reasons to explain our failures, because they shield us from anxiety and protect our self-images. Rationalization is one way we reduce cognitive dissonance and make our thoughts harmonize with our actions. If you turn back to Chapter Three, you will find the smoker rationalizing his way to harmony.

We feel foolish if we act without some reason. Howard and Tracy Kendler described a hypnotized person who had been told in his trance that after he awoke he was to raise the window whenever he saw the hypnotist take a handkerchief from his pocket. The hypnotist also told the subject that he would forget that he had ever received the instruction. Later, when the hypnosis experiment was supposed to be over and the subject was talking to friends, the hypnotist took out his handkerchief. The subject immediately walked to the window. He hesitated, not knowing why he was about to open the window, but at last he threw open the glass and said, "Isn't it a little stuffy in here?" He had found his reason.

Sometimes we deny our forbidden impulses with *reaction formation*. We convince ourselves that we want just the opposite of the dangerous goal. A mother who did not really want her child showers it with attention; a man who fears his sexual impulses becomes a crusader against pornography; a person who is drawn to cruelty forms a society to protect animals — but then says that he thinks people who mistreat animals should be tortured or killed. Reaction-formation often betrays itself by a person's intense dedication to the substitute goal.

We can also retreat from a threatening reality through *regression*. When anxiety becomes unbearable, we return to a form of behavior that we have outgrown. One of the commonest cases of regression is the three- or four-year-old who starts wetting his bed or sucking his thumb when a new baby arrives.

Instead of fleeing, a person can also ease his frustrations by emphasizing a desirable trait. This is called *compensation*, because the behavior a person emphasizes makes up for the failure that causes him anxiety. Sometimes an unattractive boy or girl will work hard to develop a sparking personality. A man with an unimportant job may become the Grand Imperial Potentate of a secret lodge. The boy who cannot make the football team may become a sports writer.

Compensation can often be helpful, but not always. A man may compensate for his inferior job by becoming a bully at home. A lonely, unloved person may stuff himself with food until he is dangerously overweight.

Sublimation is a special form of compensation. The person who sublimates expresses his sexual feelings or his aggression in ways that society finds praiseworthy. Freud believed that artists and writers create their paintings, their sculpture, their poems, and their novels by sublimating their sexual drives. A simpler example is the aggressive person who becomes a surgeon or a literary critic; another, the juvenile delinquent who finds that society will allow him to fight if he becomes a professional boxer.

Perhaps the commonest defense mechanism of all is *fantasy*. When we want something we cannot have, we relieve our anxieties by daydreaming about our desires. A young girl will daydream about the beautiful horse she cannot have; a young boy may daydream about playing quarterback for the New York Jets.

Almost everyone daydreams frequently. Several psychologists have studied fantasy and, in each case, found that about 97 percent of their subjects had recently daydreamed.

Fantasy is harmful only when our imaginary exploits stand in the way of our accomplishments in the real world. If the law student's daydreams about pleading a case before the Supreme Court keep him from studying and he fails his bar examination, his fantasies have harmed him. But the law student with the same daydream who studies hard to make his fantasies come true has been helped by his flights of imagination.

A knowledge of frustration and the ways in which people cope with it makes it easier for us to understand and accept behavior that seems stupid or mean or nonsensical. There is nothing wrong in using defense mechanisms. When we use them properly, we shift from one mechanism to another as we meet different frustrations. When we use defense mechanisms improperly, we become rigid and cling to the same defense in every situation, no matter how inappropriate it may be.

We could get along without our defenses only in a society in which our every wish was gratified the moment we felt it. Obviously, all of us want things we cannot have and have impulses that neither society nor our consciences will allow us to express.

Defense mechanisms allow us to survive in a world full of frustrations. They enable whole societies to survive during times of war. They are bad when they keep us from solving our problems or when they distort reality until they interfere with our living satisfying lives.

Persuasion

11

O N THE FIRST DAY of school, an unusual student showed up in the speech class at Oregon State University. He was clad in a big black bag that hid every part of him except his feet and his arms. The bag was tied above his head, and his eyes peered out through tiny holes. Only the instructor, Charles Goetzinger, knew who this student was.

At first the other members of the class disliked the Black Bag. For the first four weeks of class, the other students pretended that the Black Bag did not exist. They did not speak to him, would not sit next to him in class, and when Goetzinger gave the students a chance to talk about the problem, they refused to discuss the Bag. Once when the Black Bag came into class and sat down next to a young man, the man poked him with an umbrella, told him to get away, then moved to another part of the room. The classroom was always tense and tempers were short.

Then one day a class member gave a speech that described how the Black Bag disturbed him. Now the class could talk about the Bag and, even more important, they could talk *to* the Bag. Gradually the atmosphere began to change. Instead of hating the Black Bag, his classmates accepted and even liked him.

As the news of the Black Bag spread through the campus,

the town, and across the country, the class began to watch over the Bag. They defended him to outsiders and protected him from the newspaper reporters and television cameras. At last, all hostility was gone. Even the members of the community began to talk proudly about "our Black Bag."

The black bag was a psychological experiment, an experiment to explore people's attitudes and the way they change. We all have attitudes, favorable and unfavorable — about butterflies, snakes, spinach, pizza, blacks, Wall Street brokers, Roman Catholics, the Republican party, Christmas, Paul Newman, and God. These attitudes are curious jumbles of ideas, beliefs, habits, and motives that we associate with everything around us.

For example, Susan has an extremely favorable attitude toward pizza. She likes it. She knows that pizza is a combination of tomato sauce, spices, cheese — and any number of other ingredients, from anchovies to sausage — baked on a thin dough crust. She believes that it has a great number of calories. She expects that its taste will be pleasant. And she acts on this mixture of knowledge, belief, and expectation: she has a habit of eating it late at night after a football game or a movie. But because of her belief in the caloric content of pizza, she always refuses a second piece.

Psychologists are interested in two things about attitudes: how we form them and how we change them. Before we can form an attitude, we must be able to distinguish one object or person from another. For example, Ralph Rosnow has traced the formation of one attitude — a white child's prejudice against blacks.

Unless a child grows up in a biracial neighborhood, he will be three or four years old before he notices any difference in skin color. When he first notices that all human skin is not the same shade, he makes no judgment on the differences, but merely recognizes that they exist.

Once the child notices that this difference exists, he begins to relate various groups of stimuli. He notices that certain kinds of facial features accompany skin color, and that persons with different skins have different ways of talking and acting.

He soon begins to attach positive or negative emotions to each group. Somehow, black becomes bad and white becomes good. He listens to his parents, he picks up the careless remarks of his sitter, the inflection of his teacher's voice, the casual intolerance of the man next door. He may show his negative feelings by complaining that a black child in his kindergarten class "always has a black face." Now he rapidly moves into a hardened attitude. He understands the message of many books, magazines, and television programs that black is not as good as white. Even the fact that the cowboy hero always wears white and the rustler dresses in black is not lost on him. He accepts the stereotypes of his culture and, if he has little contact with blacks, most of his experiences reinforce those stereotypes.

But attitudes can change. If the prejudiced white child meets blacks under favorable circumstances, his attitudes will begin to shift. Studies of housing projects have shown that when blacks and whites live together in integrated buildings, attitudes change.

As new projects opened, M. Deutsch and M. E. Collins interviewed housewives before they moved in and rated them on the degree of their prejudice toward other races. After whites and blacks had lived together in the same buildings for a time, Deutsch and Collins rated them again. They found that over 70 percent of the most prejudiced white women had changed in their behavior and their attitudes. Now they were friendly with black women. The attitudes of black housewives had shifted in the same way. Meeting people of other races had made prejudices crumble.

Once more we have come upon a familiar topic: *cognitive dissonance*. When the women in the housing project began meeting women of other races in the laundry room and in the halls, and when their children began playing together, they entered a state of cognitive dissonance. They believed one way and acted another. They could no longer reconcile their prejudices with their own actions. It's hard to have cake and coffee with someone and still profess to hate her race. The only way for these women to get out of their unpleasant state was to change either their beliefs or their actions. They either had to give up their prejudices or stop seeing their new friends, which meant they would live isolated, unhappy lives.

Cognitive dissonance is the first step in attitude change. And one way to bring it about is to put a person into a situation that requires him to act in a way that conflicts with his usual attitudes or behavior.

In another study, a group of boys became part of a psychological experiment on attitudes and behavior. Muzafer Sherif and a team of social psychologists arranged a set of unusual conditions at a summer camp for boys near Robbers Cave, Oklahoma. The subjects were all healthy, normal boys from middle-class homes, and not one of them knew that a group of psychologists were watching their every move that summer.

From the very beginning, the boys were kept in two separate groups. They came to the camp in different buses; they lived in separate cabins; they swam, hiked, and played games only with members of their own group. Each group had its own name: one was called the Eagles; the other, the Rattlers.

After the psychologists were sure that the boys had developed a sense of belonging to their own bands, they set up a competition. By pitting the Eagles against the Rattlers in a series of baseball and football games, tugs-of-war, and treasure hunts, they turned the groups into two hostile nations. There was name-calling and scuffling.

The Eagles burned the Rattlers' banner, and that was the signal for a series of raids on each other's cabins. When a member of one group tried to make peace between the two bands, the rest of his group refused to talk to him and excluded him from activities whenever they could.

The psychologists staged a good-will dinner to see if mere contact would affect the boys' attitudes. The Eagles and Rattlers pushed each other, threw food, and shouted insults. As Sherif had predicted, neither shared dinners nor shared movies changed attitudes or behavior.

Now Sherif and his team manipulated events so the boys would have to cooperate. They cut the pipeline that brought water into the camp, and the Eagles and Rattlers had to work together to repair the system. They had the driver run a truck loaded with food for an overnight hike into a ditch. To get the truck back onto the road, the boys had to pull together on a tow rope. Gradually, the Eagles and the Rattlers became friends. When it was time to leave camp, the boys asked to ride home on the same bus.

Competition made the Eagles think that the Rattlers were sneaks and cheaters; cooperation made them into good guys. The boys were the same; the social conditions were different.

Psychologists are not the only persons interested in how attitudes change. Governments, politicians, and companies with products to sell have a keen interest in learning how to change attitudes, because when attitudes change, behavior may change, too. When the government tries to change our attitudes, we call it propaganda; when a manufacturer tries to change them, we call it advertising.

When the President of the United States makes a television speech explaining a new and perhaps unpopular policy, he is attempting to persuade you that his decision to adopt a new course in foreign affairs or inflation control was a wise one. The chances are that he will succeed. Many studies of direct attempts to change attitudes show that persuasion is likely to work if the listener believes that the persuader is trustworthy and that he knows what he is talking about.

Nearly forty years ago, I. Lorge asked Americans to read the following statement: "I hold that a little rebellion, now and then, is a good thing, and as necessary in the political world as storms are in the physical." When readers believed that Thomas Jefferson, one of our founding fathers, wrote the statement, they tended to agree with it. When they believed that V. I. Lenin, one of the founding fathers of the Soviet government, wrote the statement, they tended to disagree with it.

Lorge checked into the political attitudes of his readers and found that the more a reader respected the political philosophy of Jefferson or of Lenin, the more enthusiastically he supported the statement.

Years later, after World War II, students in advanced history courses at Yale University again showed the importance of the source in persuading people to change their minds. C. I. Hovland and W. Weiss worked one-sided statements on controversial questions into regular history lectures. Sometimes they indicated that the statement came from a trustworthy source; at other times they said that the information came from a source they knew the students would not trust. By presenting the messages during regular class lectures, they kept the students from finding out that they were part of an attitude-change experiment.

Once, for example, they discussed atomic submarines, which did not exist at the time of the study. The instructor argued that atomic submarines could, indeed, be built. On half the occasions he backed up his statement, by saying that J. Robert Oppenheimer, the nuclear physicist and one of the fathers of the atomic bomb, supported his view. The rest of the time he said that *Pravda,* the Soviet newspaper, supported it.

Great numbers of the students who had heard that Oppenheimer — whose judgment they trusted — believed in the atomic submarine said that they, too, believed that one day nations would build atomic subs. Only a few of the students who had heard that *Pravda* supported the submarine's practicality said that they believed in the future of such submarines.

But when Hovland and Weiss retested the students four weeks later, a curious thing had happened. Many of the students who had been convinced by Oppenheimer's reputation no longer believed that atomic submarines were possible. And many of the students who had not been swayed by *Pravda's* endorsement now believed that atomic submarines could be built. Apparently, as time passed the students separated the information from the source. There was now little difference between the two groups. They judged the practicality of the submarine on the information itself and not on the trustworthiness of the source.

Psychologists call this the *sleeper effect,* and other studies have shown that it is a common factor in attitude change. Later research indicates that if a person is reminded of the original information source, the power of that source again operates on his attitude. Advertisers know this, and that is why,

after you see Joe Namath endorse an electric razor on television, you will find a smiling photograph of Namath next to the
razor display in the corner drugstore.

Simply seeing or hearing something over and over again
helps to change a person's attitude. Robert Zajonc (rhymes
with "science") bought a small ad in the college newspapers at
the University of Michigan and Michigan State University.
Every day for several weeks his ad consisted of words in
Turkish like *iktitaf, biwouni,* and *civadra.* Some of the words
appeared only once, some appeared twice, others five, ten, or
twenty-five times.

After the ads stopped running, Zajonc visited several classes
on each campus. Without mentioning the advertising campaign, he gave the list to the students and told them that the
words were Turkish adjectives. Some of the words, he said,
had good meanings, while others had bad meanings. He asked
the students to guess whether each word on the list had a
good or a bad meaning. He also mailed questionnaires to
hundreds of the newspapers' subscribers, asking them to do
the same.

In every group, the words that Zajonc advertised the most
were considered good, and the ones he advertised least were
guessed to be bad. Merely seeing words each day on a page of
the campus newspaper had made the students like them.

Even rats prefer the familiar. H. A. Cross, C. G. Halcomb,
and W. W. Matter divided baby rats into three groups. The
first group spent fifty-two days listening to music by Mozart.
For twelve hours each day they heard Mozart concertos and
symphonies. The second group spent its twelve hours a day
for fifty-two days listening to music by Schönberg. The third
group heard no music at all.

At the end of the fifty-two days, the psychologists gave the rats a rest. For two weeks, none of them heard music. Then each rat was tested in a special cage. The floor was wired so that if a rat was in one half of the cage, his weight tripped a switch that started a Mozart tape. If he moved to the other side of the cage, his weight triggered a tape filled with Schönberg selections.

The rats that had grown up to the strains of Mozart preferred the Mozart side of the cage; the rats who had spent fifty-two days with Schönberg liked the Schönberg side better. The control group of rats divided their time between the two sides, but spent a little more time on the Mozart side than on the Schönberg side.

The two kinds of music are very different. Mozart's music is filled with harmonious, easily followed melody; Schönberg's compositions are difficult and discordant to untrained ears. Yet mere exposure to Schönberg — whose music many concert-goers find hard to like or understand — was enough to turn rats into Schönberg fans.

But exposure is not the only way to change attitudes. As with every other aspect of our lives, our attitudes are closely tied up with our emotions. Ads on television, on billboards, in newspapers and in magazines hint that if we will only switch our brands of toothpaste or mouthwash or deodorant, the opposite sex will find us impossible to resist.

Few people, for example, leave their emotions at home when they buy new cars. Most of us choose cars that fit our images of the ideal and pay no attention to such matters as mileage, cost of spare parts, and durability. A few years ago, not many young people bought Dodge cars. Dodge television advertisements featured a spry grandmother who urged the viewer, "Put a Dodge in your garage, honey." To make matters worse, Dodge sponsored the Lawrence Welk show, which had little appeal to youthful viewers. To break into the youth market, Dodge had to get rid of its stodgy image. The manufacturers hired a beautiful blonde model and launched the "Dodge Rebellion" to convince the public that young swingers drove Dodge cars. Same car, different image.

Not all emotions are positive, and not all propaganda and advertising aims at our desires. We also fear and hate, and politicians, advertisers, and other organizations sometimes play upon our negative emotions. Some congressmen have won elections by manipulating the voters' fears. They imply that their opponent is either disloyal or a well-meaning dupe of Communism. Even pitches aimed at our wants can also stir our fears. A girl who sees an Ultra-Brite ad ("gives your smile sex appeal") and switches toothpaste to attract a handsome halfback may also be afraid that she will get stuck with the creep who sits across the aisle in history if she doesn't.

The courts and public-health agencies often focus on our fears in their attempts to persuade us to act in our own best interests. Judges force traffic violaters to watch movies of bloody highway accidents in the hope that the sight of mangled bodies will scare offenders into obeying traffic laws.

Some psychologists have wondered if frightening a person does indeed change his attitudes and behavior. Howard Leventhal found in a series of experiments that fear did change attitudes and behavior. But he also found that some people kept on smoking cigarettes when they feared lung cancer or driving recklessly after they watched movies of gruesome traffic accidents.

In a set of experiments at state fairs, Leventhal had a barker attract large audiences for special health-education programs. One group heard a talk in which the speaker recommended that everyone should stop smoking and have chest x rays. The

speaker did not try to frighten this low-fear group. The mod-
erate-fear group heard the talk, then saw a movie about a
young man who learned that his chest x ray had turned up
lung cancer. People in the high-fear group heard the same
talk and saw the same movie, but Leventhal added a second
movie for their benefit. It showed a lung-cancer operation in
vivid color.

In each group, the subjects filled out questionnaires. Mobile
x-ray units on the fairground offered free x rays to all.
Leventhal checked with the x-ray unit to find out how many
of the subjects had had chest x rays, then phoned and wrote
the subjects to find out how many had stopped smoking.

When he checked the results, Leventhal found that people
in the high-fear group were not necessarily the ones who had
had chest x rays and stopped smoking. Instead, the people
who were most frightened — *in any group* — were the most
likely to take steps to preserve their health. What Leventhal
had planned as the most fearful program did not always scare
people the most. Some people in the low-fear group were
more frightened than some who saw the filmed surgery. And
some people apparently kept on smoking cigarettes even
though they feared lung cancer.

Leventhal conducted more studies. In one set of experiments he tried to persuade people to have tetanus innocula-
tions. In another, he used movies of automobile accidents to
persuade people to drive safely. He discovered that another
factor entered into the way people responded: their self-esteem. He found that persons who had high opinions of themselves were more likely to change their attitudes after hearing
about the dangers of smoking or of tetanus or of reckless driving than persons who thought little of themselves. Perhaps a
person with a low opinion of himself believes that his life is

worth little and there's no reason to preserve it. Another possibility is that low self-esteem makes people feel powerless. A person who lacks power believes that nothing he does will change his future. So he doesn't try.

Not all researchers agree with Leventhal's theories. In his own experiments, Irving Janis found that moderate doses of fear are more likely to change behavior than strong doses of fear. He believes that too much fear can make people so anxious that they become hostile and reject the message. Or perhaps they associate the fear with the message and, in order to reduce their anxiety, forget the warning.

Janis believes that empathy (identifying with another's situation) is just as important as self-esteem in changing both attitudes and behavior. Janis and Leo Mann conducted a study with twenty-six young women smokers. Not one of them intended to stop smoking cigarettes. Janis and Mann divided these women into two groups. Each person in the first group was asked to play the part of a patient with lung cancer in an hour-long scene with one of the researchers. The researcher wore a white lab coat, showed the woman a chest x ray, described the cancer he spotted on the film, and told her that all tests showed that she must have immediate surgery. Then, while the "doctor" was arranging for her operation, the woman described, as part of her role, how she felt about her disease and the prospect of surgery.

The other group of women had no chance to play the role of the cancer patient. Instead, they listened to a tape recording of one of the hour-long sessions. After the experiment, cigarette smoking dropped sharply in both groups of women, but the women who had taken the part of the cancer victim smoked fewer cigarettes each day than the ones who had merely listened to the recording. Eighteen months later Janis and Mann checked both groups again. Cigarette consumption was still down in each group, and the "actresses" still smoked significantly fewer cigarettes each day than the other women did.

Janis thinks that playing the role of the victim lowers a person's resistance to a persuasive message, because she experiences the same feelings she would have in the victim's situation. In other words, the actor empathizes with the victim. Janis points out that Leventhal had used movies of a young cancer victim in his experiments. These movies, says Janis, probably caused the audience to empathize with the cancer patient in the film. According to Janis, their empathy, not their self-esteem, lowered their resistance to the message presented by the speaker.

Society plays a large role in the formation of our attitudes. Especially important to us are the attitudes of our friends and acquaintances. The part that groups play in shaping our attitudes and behavior interests many psychologists.

This country went through a meat shortage during World War II, and the government asked families to eat meatless meals once or twice each week in order to stretch the supply of roasts, steaks, chops, and hamburger. But there was always a plentiful supply of hearts, brains, sweetbreads, and kidneys in the butcher shops, simply because most housewives don't serve these meats.

Kurt Lewin had the job of developing a one-hour program that would encourage women to feed their families these nutritious but unpopular meats. He set up two programs. In one, a lecturer told the women that eating these meats would aid the war effort. He also spoke about their nutritional value and described delicious meals that could be made from them.

The second program was a group discussion led by a person

who gave the same information that the lecturer had covered in his talk. During the program, the leader asked the women to think of reasons why they should not serve hearts, sweetbreads, kidneys, or brains to their families and then to think of arguments that would meet their own objections. After the discussion he asked them to raise their hands if they were willing to cook one of the meats during the next week.

A week later, Lewin checked on the women who attended both programs. Only 3 percent of the women who heard the lecture had served one of the unpopular meats to her family, while 32 percent of the women in the discussion group had served them.

There are several reasons for the effectiveness of the discussion program. First, the women thought about and discussed opinions different from their own. By answering her own objections to serving kidneys, a woman helped to change her attitude toward the meat. Second, each woman who raised her hand at the end of the discussion had publicly committed herself to trying the meat. And last, by discussing the meats in a group, the women could see that others were in favor of trying the unpopular food. By serving one of the meats, she conformed to what she believed was the standard of the group.

Most of us conform to the standards of those around us. Once we find that most of the people we know feel a certain way about a style of dress or a proposed law or a new boy in town, we are likely to shift our own attitudes closer to the attitudes of our group. It is often easier to break the rules of society than it is to go against the attitudes of our own circle of friends and acquaintances.

The pressure of group opinion showed clearly in a series of experiments by Solomon Asch. Asch set up groups of eight college students and told them that they were part of a perception experiment. He showed them a series of lines, and each of the students had to judge which line in a cluster of three matched the length of a given line. This is a simple perception test, and when people take it by themselves, they rarely make mistakes.

What one of the students did not know was that he was the only subject in the group; the other seven students were confederates of Asch. Each time the lines were shown, Asch asked the seven stooges, one by one, for their opinions before he asked the subject for his. In these experiments, one third of the subjects refused to believe the evidence of their eyes. When the seven stooges said that an obviously shorter or longer line matched the test line, one out of three subjects agreed with them.

The results that Asch got in this experiment were usually not examples of attitude change. A few of the subjects did come to believe that their eyes were playing tricks on them, but most of the students who gave in to the majority opinion said that they went along with the rest of the group because they did not want to be different.

Once again, it was shown that society has a tremendous effect on the behavior of individuals. The rewards and punishments of a lifetime teach people to comply automatically with the practices and opinions of those around them. Physicians report with alarm that each year many people quietly choke to death in restaurants. It seems that some individuals would rather die than make a fuss and break society's code for dining in public.

Society could not function without our automatic obedience to most of its rules. But there is a hidden danger in sheeplike, unthinking conformity in all things at all times. When Stanley

Milgram asked people to deliver lethal electric shocks, 65 percent of his subjects gave what they thought were deadly jolts of current when it appeared that society had okayed the procedure.

When the traffic light flashes red, your life depends upon complying without thought to the rules. But when you are asked to disbelieve the evidence before you or to violate the rights of others, it is time for you to test the facts and to make your own decisions.

If you can spot the ways, the techniques others use to persuade you to buy their products, to vote for their candidates, or to follow their personal desires and wishes, you will have more control over your own life. You will be able to pick your way through this bombardment — the blandishments, the promises, and the simple solutions you find in newspapers, magazines, movies, and television. Because you understand the way your thoughts and feelings work, you can be a competent consumer — and a better, more responsible citizen.

Glossary

ACETYLCHOLINE: one of the chemicals that transmit impulses between neurons

ACTUALIZE: Carl Rogers' term for the organism's attempts to improve and grow and become independent

ADRENALINE: a chemical that prepares the body for quick action. It is produced by the adrenal glands and also by the neurons. Also called epinephrine

AGGRESSION: hostile or destructive behavior, by word or by action

AMBIVERT: a person whose personality shows a mixture of introversion and extraversion

ANTHROPOLOGY: the scientific study of the origins, development, customs, and behavior of human beings

ANXIETY: a fear that seems to have no specific cause

APPROACH-APPROACH CONFLICT: a conflict that arises when a person or animal wants two goals, but satisfying one means losing the other

APPROACH-AVOIDANCE CONFLICT: a conflict that arises when a person or animal wants a goal but at the same time is repelled by it

ASSOCIATIONAL THINKING: a relaxed, nonlogical flow of ideas, as in daydreams or nightdreams; also called divergent thinking

ATTITUDE: a mixture of ideas, beliefs, habits, and motives that predisposes a person to respond consistently to ideas, objects, persons, or issues. Attitudes are learned and may be favorable or unfavorable

AUTHORITARIAN PERSON: one who believes in absolute obedience to authority and who, therefore, needs to follow a strong leader

AVOIDANCE-AVOIDANCE CONFLICT: a conflict that arises when a person or animal must choose between two courses of action, both of which are distasteful

AVOIDANCE DRIVE: a drive that is reduced when the person or animal escapes from unpleasant stimulation; also called an aversive drive

AXON: the long trunk of the neuron that carries impulses away from the main part of the cell

BEHAVIORISM: the school of psychology that limits its study to the behavior of man and animals. Behaviorists do not study "mind" or "consciousness" or "feelings"; they are interested only in behavior they can observe and measure

BEHAVIOR GENETICS: the scientific study of inherited behavior

CELL ASSEMBLY: a group of neurons that form a circuit. When the circuit is stimulated, the neurons fire in sequence, triggering a memory

CHROMOSOME: threadlike bodies within cells made up of proteins, DNA, and RNA; chromosomes are always found in pairs

CLASSICAL CONDITIONING: a simple form of learning. A neutral stimulus (such as a bell) comes to stand for a potent stimulus (such as food) and brings forth the response that the person or animal usually gives to the potent stimulus

COGNITIVE DISSONANCE: a state in which a person's beliefs and actions do not match. Such a state may lead a person to distort reality

COMPENSATION: a defense mechanism whereby a person eases his frustrations by developing and emphasizing a desirable trait

CONDITIONED RESPONSE: the response (such as drooling) that, after conditioning, follows a stimulus (such as a bell) which once brought forth no such reaction

CONDITIONED STIMULUS: the stimulus (such as a bell) that, after conditioning, brings forth the response (such as drooling) that originally followed the unconditioned stimulus (such as food)

CONFLICT BEHAVIOR: behavior of a person or animal caught between conflicting wishes, goals, or drives

CONFORMITY: acting in the same way as others, or becoming like them; often the result of social pressure from one's peers

CONNOTATIVE MEANING: the associations and emotional implications of a word

CONTACT COMFORT: the pleasure that comes from cuddling with a warm, soft object

CONTROL GROUP: a group of subjects who undergo the same testing but do not have the original experience that the psychologist is studying

CULTURE: the traditional patterns of a society, including its customs, beliefs, government, and arts

CULTURE-FAIR INTELLIGENCE TEST: an intelligence test on which people of the same intelligence, no matter what culture they live in, will make identical scores

DATA: information that results from experiments, tests, surveys, and interviews

DEFENSE MECHANISM: a habit that distorts, denies, or falsifies reality in order to protect the ego

DENDRITE: one of the treelike branches of a neuron (nerve cell) which sends impulses from other neurons to the main part of the cell

DENIAL: a defense mechanism whereby a person rejects the existence of an unpleasant fact or situation

DENOTATIVE MEANING: the explicit meaning of a word

DEPRIVATION: the lack or loss of something that one wants or needs

DISPLACEMENT: a defense mechanism whereby a person shifts an idea, activity, or emotion from its proper object to some unrelated object

DRIVE: the condition of a person or animal that starts and directs his behavior

ECTOMORPH: a person with a thin, small-muscled body

EGO: "I"; usually the conscious self, but in Freud's terms, that part of the personality which controls behavior and recognizes external reality

EIDETIC MEMORY: photographic memory, in which the person re-sees the event as if it were projected onto a movie screen

ELECTRODE: a metal device that conducts electricity

EMOTION: any strong feeling such as joy, rage, fear, love, sorrow, hate, or disgust

EMPATHY: understanding another's thoughts or feelings by putting oneself into his or her situation

END-BRANCH: a rootlike ending of the axon that sends impulses to other neurons

ENDOMORPH: a person with a soft, fat, round body

ENVIRONMENT: the surroundings of any plant, person, or animal. These conditions affect both the organism's present state and its growth and development

EPILEPSY: a brain disorder that can be mild or severe. In severe cases, the victim has attacks that send him into convulsions

EXTINCTION: the disappearance of a behavior because the person or animal no longer is reinforced for producing it

EXTRAVERT: an outgoing person who responds quickly to the world around him

FANTASY: a defense mechanism whereby a person satisfies his desires by imagining that they are fulfilled

FRUSTRATION: the state of a person or animal who has been blocked and kept from reaching his goal

FUNCTIONAL FIXEDNESS: a condition that occurs when one becomes so fixed on one use of a tool or an object that he literally cannot think of using it in any other way

GENE: a unit within a chromosome which carries the specific traits that are passed from parent to child

HOLOGRAM: a three-dimensional photograph made by storing the entire scene on many points of the film

HOMEOSTASIS: a state of physiological balance which the body reaches by automatically adjusting its internal conditions

Hypothalamus: a portion of the brain containing centers which influence many drives, such as hunger or thirst

Id: Freud's term for that part of the person made up of drives, needs, and instincts. The id demands immediate satisfaction of these needs

Identification: the process of responding to a situation as if it were the same as a previous one; the process of accepting the values and purposes of another person or group for one's self

Insight: the ability to perceive the true nature of something; a new understanding that appears to come in a sudden flash

Instinct: an unlearned behavior that a person or animal performs correctly the first time the appropriate circumstances arise

Intermittent reinforcement: reinforcing a person or animal for a particular behavior for only part of the time; also called partial reinforcement

Introjection: a special form of identification in which a person takes on the qualities of his persecutor

Introvert: a quiet, shy, withdrawn person who is concerned with his own thoughts and feelings

IQ: intelligence quotient; a number score produced when one divides the score representing a person's mental age by his chronological age and then multiplies the result by 100. Intelligence tests are constructed so that persons of average intelligence will make IQ scores of 90–110.

Isolation: a defense mechanism whereby a person accepts unpleasant facts or situations intellectually but blocks out the emotions that normally accompany those facts

Latent learning: learning that takes place without any response by the person or animal, and for which the person or animal receives no reward

Long-term memory: memory that lasts for days, months, years, or even for a person's entire life

Maze: a series of small alleys, some leading to exits or to food and others ending in blind walls. Mazes are used in laboratories to test the learning and motivation of animals

Mesomorph: a person whose body has powerful muscles and prominent bones

Mnemonics: devices, such as formulas or rhymes, that help one to remember

Motivation: the conditions that cause a person to perform one act rather than another

MOTIVE: the reason or emotion that causes a person to perform a particular act; this reason or emotion rests on the person or animal's expectation of the pleasant or unpleasant effects of his action

NARCOLEPSY: a disorder in which a person suddenly falls into a deep sleep

NATURE-NURTURE CONTROVERSY: the argument as to whether heredity (the traits passed along in one's genes) or environment (one's surroundings and experiences) is responsible for personality, intelligence, or behavior

NEGATIVE REINFORCEMENT: any stimulus (such as electric shock) whose removal makes it more likely that the animal or person will repeat his behavior

NEURON: any cell in the central nervous system

NORM: a custom so important to a society that people who follow it are rewarded and people who break it are punished

OPERANT CONDITIONING: a form of learning in which an animal or person's actions are either reinforced or punished; also called instrumental conditioning

OVERLEARNING: the fixing of information in one's memory by continuing to practice after one appears to have learned

PARANOIA: a form of psychosis in which a person has logically consistent, but bizarre delusions

PERCEPTION: the awareness of the environment brought about by interpreting sensory data such as sound, smell, sight, taste, and touch

PERSONALITY: the traits and characteristic behavior that distinguish one person from another

PERSUASION: the process of causing a person to do or to believe something

PHYSIOLOGY: the scientific study of the functions and processes of living things

POSITIVE REINFORCEMENT: any stimulus (such as food) whose presentation makes it more likely that the animal or person will repeat his behavior

PRIMARY REINFORCER: anything, such as food or water, that without any training strengthens a behavior. Primary reinforcers normally reduce homeostatic drives

PROJECTION: a defense mechanism whereby a person blames his own mistakes, failures, and unacceptable thoughts or feelings on someone or something else

PSYCHIATRIST: a physician who specializes in the medical study and treatment of mental disorders

PSYCHOANALYSIS: a system of therapy originated by Sigmund Freud that helps a person overcome severe guilt and anxiety by exploring his childhood, dreams, mental processes, and behavior. Today most psychoanalysts are also psychiatrists, which means that they have first been trained as medical doctors

PSYCHOLOGY: the scientific study of behavior

PSYCHOSIS: a severe mental disorder in which a person can no longer deal effectively with reality

PUNISHMENT: a penalty that follows behavior and makes it less likely that a person or animal will repeat the behavior

RATIONALIZATION: a defense mechanism whereby a person concocts plausible reasons to explain his behavior or beliefs

REACTION FORMATION: a defense mechanism whereby a person develops conscious attitudes which are directly opposite to threatening or forbidden desires

REGRESSION: a defense mechanism whereby a person under severe stress returns to an earlier, immature form of thinking and behavior

REHEARSAL: the repetition of information or behavior that one wishes to learn. Rehearsal helps to transfer information from short-term memory to long-term memory

REINFORCER: something that makes it more likely that an animal or person will repeat the action that came before the reinforcer

REPLICATE: to repeat an experiment in order to see if the same procedure will produce similar results

REPRESSION: a way of avoiding guilt or anxiety by pushing certain memories out of one's conscious mind

RETROGRADE AMNESIA: the inability to remember events that took place just before an injury, even though memory of earlier events remains clear

SAMPLE: a representative group used to study the attitudes or behavior of a larger group

SECONDARY REINFORCER: something that, because it has become associated with a primary reinforcer, strengthens a behavior

SELF: what the person means when he thinks "I" or "me"

SELF-ACTUALIZATION: the process of fulfilling one's potentials; the state of the fully developed person

SELF-ESTEEM: a sense of one's own worth

SENSORY DEPRIVATION: an experimental procedure that isolates people from stimulation for a long period

SET: a tendency to use a single way of solving a problem based on one's previous experience

SHORT-TERM MEMORY: memory that lasts only a few seconds after one is exposed to information

SLEEPER EFFECT: a term that refers to the diminishing effect of authority or prestige as time passes and the person separates the information from the prestigious source

SOCIOLOGY: the scientific study of human society and its institutions

STATE-DEPENDENT LEARNING: learning that is linked to one's physical condition at the time one learns the response. Alcohol, tranquilizers, and barbiturates can produce state-dependent learning

STEREOTYPE: a preconceived and oversimplified opinion, belief, or idea about a person, group, event, or issue; a person or thing without individual characteristics, made to conform to the observer's fixed ideas

STIMULUS: some event or object that causes a person or animal to react; the stimulus may be in the outside environment or within the person or animal

SUBLIMATION: a defense mechanism whereby a person transforms his sexual urges or his aggression into praiseworthy behavior

SUPEREGO: Freud's term for a partly conscious part of the ego that picks up standards of morality and uses them to hold back the id; the conscience

SYNAPSE: the place between neurons where the end-branches of one nerve cell transmit impulses to the dendrites of another

TRAIT: a distinctive feature of a person or animal

TRANSMITTER CHEMICAL: a chemical such as acetylcholine, epinephrine, or norepinephrine that transmits impulses between the cells in the central nervous system

UNCONDITIONED STIMULUS: the original, potent stimulus (such as food) that brings forth a response (such as drooling) in classical conditioning

Index

Acetylcholine, use of, in experiments, 63–64

Achievement, impact on society of strong need for, 44–45

Actualization, defined, 133–34

Adjustment, 141–53

Adorno, T. W., 129

Adrenal glands: impact of emotions on, 49, 50; use of epinephrine from, 64

Advertising, role of, in changing attitudes, 159–60, 161–62, 163–64

Aesop, 150

Affiliation motive, 46–47

Aggression: defined, 51; and frustration, 51–53, 144–45; and pain, 54; theory of learned, 60; use of electricity to increase, 61–63; displaced, 147–48

Alcohol, effect of, on memory, 94

Alcoholics, 39, 47

Alike and *different*, ability of monkeys to learn concepts of, 76

Ambiverts, defined, 128

American Heritage School Dictionary, The, 105

Amnesia, retrograde, 91

Anger, leading to aggression, 51–52, 144–45

Anglos, view of nature by, contrasted with Navajos, 118

Animals, attempts to teach language to, 111–15

Anthropology, defined, 17

Anxiety, 56–57, 146

Approach-approach conflict, 142, 143

Approach-avoidance conflict, 142, 144

Aroused state, 35–36

Asch, Solomon, 168–69

Associational thinking, 102–3, 105

Atkinson, Richard, 77

Attitudes: formation and changing of, 156–58; psychological experiment on, 158–59; efforts to influence, through propaganda and advertising, 159–64; link between emotions and, 163–67; role of society in formation of, 167–70

Authoritarian personality type, described, 129–30

Automobile, impact on American society of, 29

Avoidance (or aversive drive), 39–40, 54

Avoidance-avoidance conflict, 142, 143–44

Axon, of neurons, 82

Azrin, Nathan, 54

Bagby, J. W., 20

Bandura, Albert, 53, 60

Barriers, to achieving goals, 141–42

Baxter, J. C., 121

Beethoven, Ludwig van, 134

Behavior geneticists, 25

Behaviorism, 68

Bennett, E. L., 108

Binet, Alfred, 105

Birch, Herbert G., 98–99, 100

"Black Bag" (a psychological experiment), 155–56